WALKING WITH
Clarence

WALKING WITH
Clarence

JED ALLEN FREELS

A Sacred Journey To A Deeper Faith

authorHOUSE®

AuthorHouse™
1663 Liberty Drive
Bloomington, IN 47403
www.authorhouse.com
Phone: 1-800-839-8640

First published by AuthorHouse   10/20/2011

ISBN: 978-1-4670-4447-9 (sc)
ISBN: 978-1-4670-4446-2 (hc)
ISBN: 978-1-4670-4448-6 (ebk)

Library of Congress Control Number: 2011919808

Printed in the United States of America

Any people depicted in stock imagery provided by Thinkstock are models, and such images are being used for illustrative purposes only.
Certain stock imagery © *Thinkstock.*

This book is printed on acid-free paper.

For

Clarence

Special Thanks
To:

Family and Friends, who have the willingness and the faith to believe.
My wife, Keli, for always being by my side.
Austin, Cody, and Carrie for being there to help me see simple truths.
Mom & Dad, for being the safe harbor I can always come home to.
Kathie, Barb, & Marlene for being a great advisory team.
and
John Romaine for providing a sanctuary where Walking With
Clarence was written.

Contents

Prologue: Looking For Directions

It is not easy to talk about something when people will say, "No Way!" It is not easy to write about something when people will say, "Impossible!" It is not easy to tell a story that spans almost thirty-five years and expect people to believe you, especially when it involves something they themselves may have never experienced and possibly never will. Yet it is a story that I know now I must continue to tell.

I do not know why God keeps a close eye on me. Maybe I am a soul on the edge, and he is afraid of losing me. Maybe I need lots of extra guidance to reach my destination and fulfill my own journey. Maybe I attempt to do so many things that I just cannot get them all done with out a little help from HIM.

I believe that everyone has guardian angels that are constantly at work for them. Some of them are everyday people who we walk and work with each and every day. Some of them are people we may meet only once, yet they will impact our lives in an enormous way forever. Sometimes they are of the spiritual type. We feel their presence and hear their voices. Sometimes they walk beside us in our times of need and in joy. The problem is that most of the time we are all too busy to sense their presence. We do not take time to look for the angels among us and observe their helping hands.

This is my story as I have traveled on a sacred journey in the hands of God.

Chapter 1 Pushing the limits

The Hobie Cat

As the storm intensified and the swelling waves continued to push us towards shore, I realized that time was of the essence. Our continued attempts at righting the Hobie had proved unsuccessful. As Lake Michigan continued to unleash her mighty forces, I began to comprehend that this could be the end. Laying my head on the overturned tramp, I began to pray . . . .

6 Hours earlier

It was a beautiful day on the southern shores of Lake Michigan. I had chosen to spend the summer between my sophomore and junior years of college working on my Dad's charter boat for the summer. Most days were filled with First Mate duties. The duties included things like getting up early to stow lines, check equipment, make coffee, and in general ensure that *The Country Boy* was ready for her charter that day. But today was different. *The Country Boy* was scheduled for some routine maintenance so I had the day off. When you have a day off on the southern shores of Lake Michigan, the question is not what to do. The question is just which beach to do it on. But just as luck would have it my day off was not going to be a great beach day. The skies were overcast and a northern' was blowing in. This usually meant that the next three days would be anything but picture perfect.

   The Country Boy was berthed right next to the Coast Guard station so I glanced over at the weather flags of the day ...."Huh, 2-4 footers, that's not bad." So, I guess when God gives you lemons, you make lemonade . . . time to go sailing.

   I called my buddy, Craig, and said, "What do you think about a morning sail before this storm gets too bad?" He was up for the challenge and plans were tentatively set. I called Quake to see if anyone was using the Hobie Cat that day. He said it was a little rough for most people, and the Hobie was sitting on the beach at the Red Lantern Inn. I called Craig back and said, "We're on."

   The Red Lantern Inn at that time was a great place to start a sail. It was located on the edge of the beach right in the middle of the Indiana Dunes National Lakeshore. The front of the inn at one time had been protected with a rock break wall to keep the surf from eroding the beach on which the inn was built. This made a great place for Hobie Caters to keep their boats if you could make arrangements with Danny at the inn to store your sails and equipment. Quake had connections everywhere so he had an in with Danny. The thing that was so great about having the Red Lantern as a base is you did not have a long sail out of the harbor to hit good wind and waves which is the goal of every Hobie Cater. At the Red Lantern, you just shoved off, and you were sailing.

   Quake's Hobie Cat was an orange sixteen-footer with sunburst sails, a perfect craft. Among Hobie Caters, it was the vessel of choice. A fourteen-footer could not quite handle truly rough water, and an eighteen-footer was just a little too stable and safe. If you wanted to be on the edge and push the limits, the sixteen-footer was the ride.

Craig and I arrived at the Red Lantern Inn at about the same time and surveyed the surf. It was rough, pushing three footers, but if the storm held off we should have a great morning of one-hulling. We quickly changed into our wet suits and carried the rigging equipment and sails from the Red Lantern out to the Hobie Cat. Craig attached the rudders and center boards while I attached the jib sail. Together we attached the main sail and boom and ran the main sail up the mast. Her sunburst color pattern was visible for miles down the beach, especially since we were the only people making sail. We grabbed our life vests, put them on over our wetsuits, and then secured our trapeze harnesses in place. As our final presail check, we pulled the plugs on both sides of the twin-hulled catamaran and made sure that they were water free. All was right so we replaced the plugs, swung the bow around, and shoved off.

It was a great wind to tack into with plenty of power to overcome the current level of surf. It was sure to make for some great hull running. We drew taunt the jib sail, pulled in the main mast boom, and the Hobie surged out to sea. The swells were challenging but once we broke free of the crashing surf, they were manageable. We tacked northeast for about ten minutes to get out into open water. Then we brought her about to the port side. As the boom swung and the jib adjusted, we settled in for a nice northwest tack. It was exhilarating. As we pulled in the main boom to capture more wind, the tiny craft rose out of the water. We were one-hulling. Craig and I both fastened into the trapeze harness. As the little craft stood on her side and rode the waves with her port hull, we were standing on the starboard hull a full eight feet above the water. We leaned out over the churning sea below us, attached only by the thin cable running from the mast to our trapeze harness. We were human counterbalances to keep the tiny craft from capsizing. We were on the edge, and we loved it. The morning stretched on and with each tack and change in direction, we sailed farther from shore. Caught up in the moment of each hull ride, we jumped from swell to swell and from crest to crest. We realized that the seas were becoming rougher. This added to the exhilarating feel each time one of the sixteen-foot hulls would dance up and out of the water to fly with us aboard.

Then it happened: a small slip on a starboard tack. As we came around and slid across the trampoline that connected the two sixteen-foot hulls, a gust of wind surged and caught the main sail before I could release the main boom rope from the secured position just below the main boom pulley. The Hobie surged sideways and the sail crashed into the lake. We were both attached by our safety lines, and as we slid into the lake the craft pulled us forward. I furiously kicked for the surface, with a hand instinctively above my head. I broke the surface just a few feet from the Hobie which was now lying on its side. The sails were fluttering on top of the water. I surveyed for Craig and found that he had surfaced just on the other side of the floating hull. As I joined him, we took stock of our situation. This was nothing new when you run the fine line of one-hulling. As a matter of fact, for those of us on the edge it was somewhat of a daily occurrence. We set about the simple task of righting the craft. We maneuvered the Hobie into position so that the wind would not hinder her rise. We loosened all sails and freed the tiller ropes. We stood on the floating hull and reached up for the ropes tied under the trampoline. We grabbed the rope attached to the top hull standing above the water and leaned back. As we leaned back, the weight of our bodies acted as a counterbalance. The mast and main sail began to rise out of the water. Things were going as planned just as they had every other time, on every other day when I had found myself in this situation. In a matter of minutes, we would be sailing again and pushing the limit.

Yet this time things would not go so smoothly. As the sail began to clear the water, the floating hull began to list to the stern. Quickly Craig and I walked the hull to try to balance the stern list, but we were too late. The mast dipped into the crest of an oncoming wave and sank below the surface. The stern list was too great for us to counterbalance. The mast continued to sink until our top side hull crashed into the water and joined our other floating hull. We were turtled, a Hobie Caters worst embarrassment. Our mast was pointing straight down towards the bottom of mighty Lake Michigan. We were completely upside down. Two tiny sixteen-foot hulls were attached by a trampoline, rudders and center boards pointing to the clouds paying homage to the sailing Gods. We crawled onto the upside down tramp, looked around to see if anyone could see us and laughed. No one saw us because we were so far offshore that the shoreline was a distant line on the horizon. There was not another boat in sight. Our embarrassment was safe because nobody knew but us.

We laid there on the overturned Hobie Cat for several minutes to survey the situation. The seas had become much rougher with whitecaps riding each crest now. The little craft would rise on the overturned hulls with each crest and float the troughs between each wave. The storm was definitely intensifying, and it appeared that it was time to make a break for shore.

Righting a turtled Hobie Cat was no easy task. I had done it once before in much calmer seas, but this was going to be a challenge. We positioned our weight on the port hull. Grabbing the righting lines on the bottom of the tramp, we began to lean out over the side to start the mast on the upward journey to the surface. After a few minutes, much to my satisfaction, the mast began to break free. The sail began to flap in the wind. Just as I thought we were coming over, it happened again. The hull listed to the stern, the mast dipped, caught a wave and headed back to the comfortable position pointing toward the bottom. I was perplexed, but determined. I realized the seas were rough, but this was doable. We tried again and again and again. Each time we had small variations of success but the same results. The mast pointed straight down toward the bottom of mighty Lake Michigan.

Hours passed and the seas became rougher and heavier. Without fail, every attempt to right the tiny craft so that the sunburst sails would once again fill with the northern wind were unsuccessful. It was during this time that we discovered that one of the hulls was laying low in the water. After a quick inspection, we discovered that the hull had a small breach on the keel line. The small hole was the result of being dragged up and down the beach so often. Now the picture began to come into focus. The one hull had collected just enough water during our morning sail before capsizing that she was heavy laden in the water. Every time we would try to right the craft, the water would run to the stern end of the craft and counteract our efforts. We could not drain the water from the hull because the drain plugs were on the stern surface at the bottom of the hull which of course now was the top!

With intensifying seas and what seemed an impossible task, I began to look for options. We had only two: abandon the Hobie and attempt the long swim back to shore, or stay with her and take our chances when we hit the beach.

With option one, we would be free of the Hobie. If we used our safety lines, we might be able to stay connected and both reach the beach. However in intense seas such as this, I knew the undercurrent would be strong enough to pull us both under and back out to sea. Over the years, I had witnessed my Dad pulling stranded boats off the beach and looking for people lost to the rip currents.

With option two, we could float on the Hobie and stay with her until she began to be pounded apart by the surf. That might get us close enough to overcome the undercurrents and make shore. Yet if for some reason the boat crashed and fell apart sooner we could become caught up in the debris. Reaching shore alive would be out of the question.

With neither option being acceptable, we would have to invent option three. We had to find a way to right the craft and sail her in. If we could right her in the rough seas, we could run with the wind and ride the breakers. We could land her on the beach. Determined, we started again to right the faltering Hobie Cat. We knew now that if we could counterbalance the water as it ran towards the stern, we may be able to keep her from listing. Yet when one of us would try to counter the bow to stern run of the water in the hull, the other person did not have enough counterbalances to continue righting the mast. Each time we tried to overcome the situation, we failed! We just did not have enough counterbalances in the right places at the right time to get the job done.

As we laid on the overturned trampoline with our mast still pointed to the bottom, I saw in the distance a sign of hope. This sign was the boat that I saw every morning when I woke up on *The Country Boy*, because she was docked right next to us, the US Coast Guard Cutter 44! The 44 was the toughest Coast Guard boat ever designed. She could sail straight into the oncoming waves and stand on end. She could roll completely over and right herself. She could batten down her hatches and ride out any storm if she needed to. The Coast Guard 44 was headed into port! Quickly, Craig and I jumped up and began waving. Surely they would see us. Surely the radar would pick us up. I guessed we were about two miles from shore now, still plenty far out for the 44 to make a quick pickup. Once we got too close it would be impossible for them to reach us in shallow seas. Yet the 44 kept on running for port. We waved our life vests, and jumped as high as we could with each crest. Yet with each wave that passed, the 44 sailed farther into the distance. Our turtled catamaran lying upside down in the water did not have enough of a signature in rough seas for the radar on the 44 to pick us up. What we had hoped would be a glimmering lifeline was not to be.

Now more than ever, as I laid there exhausted on the tramp, I realized our situation was worse than I had thought. If the 44 was heading in, then poorer circumstances must be looming. The conditions on the mighty lake were bound to be much worse than I expected. Now options 1 and 2 definitely seemed to end without us reaching shore alive. Option 3 was out because we just could not do it ourselves. I laid my head down to pray, but did not know what to pray for. What could God do for me that I had not already tried? What could I possibly pray for that would make a difference? Then for some reason a prayer popped into my head. It was the prayer of serenity that my mom had given me on baptism day so many years ago. It was on a little plaque that hung above my bed when I was a kid. It sat on my desk while away at college. Now it danced in my head, and I began to pray those words I had spoken so many times yet never really understood. "God Grant me the serenity to accept the things I cannot change, the courage to change the things I can, and the wisdom to know the difference." With that, a simple peace entered my soul. It was at that moment when I realized that no matter what happened I would be ok in some way. If this was the end, I needed to accept the things I could not change. Then at that very moment Craig grabbed my shoulder and screamed, "LOOK"!

My eyes were drawn in the direction he was pointing. Among the waves I saw something. It appeared to be a man swimming towards us. As the waves would crash over him he would rest. Then as the crest passed, he would swim steadily through the trough of the wave towards us. With each passing moment, he swam closer and closer until he was just a rope throw away. Grabbing one of our safety lines, I tossed him the rope which he seemed to expect. He grabbed it, and we hauled him on to the tramp beside us. There beside us sat a very fit man probably in his early sixties. He was not even winded. He wore no wet suit or life jacket and appeared to just be out for a swim. Without thinking I screamed "Are you crazy? What are you doing out here?" He simply smiled and said, "I've been watching you boys all morning and finally decided you could use a little help. Now what do you say we get this boat sailing."

Now a spirit of hope and fortitude replaced the feeling of helplessness that had been aboard the capsized Hobie just moments ago. I said "Ok, here is what we need to do . . . ." as Craig and I made our way on to the hull and grabbed the righting ropes, the man moved with grace and ease. He knew what to do before we even told him. As Craig and I began to right the Hobie and the mast started to break plane and show itself through the water, the hull began to list as it had done so many times before. Yet, this time the man quickly placed himself at the perfect counter point, and we continued an upward motion with the mast. It was working; we were coming over. As the damaged hull labored to keep us afloat, the solid hull splashed down into the water in the restored position.

Like a man who had lived on the high seas, our new companion leaped to the righted tramp and grabbed the tiller. Craig and I pulled ourselves onto the tramp with the use of our safety lines just in time to see the man at the tiller grab the main boom line and tighten the sail. We were moving. We were sailing with the wind. The damaged hull was holding us back, and in my heart I had my doubts if it would carry us over the next crest. Looking into the man's eyes I knew just what to do. I said "keep her moving, I'll pull the plug." The man simply nodded. As I leaned over the stern of the damaged hull and pulled the plug, the water began running out of the hull. As a kid, I always remembered my dad emptying the fishing boat this way when we did not feel like bailing. The forward movement of the boat always forced the moving water out the hole in the back. It was simple physics. As long as the breach in the hull was smaller than the drain hole in the stern and we kept a forward motion, the hull should become self-bailing. Sure enough, just like that little fishing boat, the hull began to empty and ride higher in the water. We were moving, and while it would not be a relaxing sail, we could ride these waves in and beach her if we did not push too hard. Our friend seemed to sense our determination returning, and he handed me the tiller bar and main line.

Then without a moment's hesitation he said, "You boys will be fine now," and over the side he dove. I panicked. He had no wet suit or life jacket. We were less than a mile off shore, and the surf was pounding. The undercurrents would be strong and no swimmer would make it through. Feverishly, I ripped my life vest off and threw it to the man, but he did not grab it. He simply turned and above the roar of the churning sea I heard him say, "Don't worry. I'll be fine," and away he swam. He rested as the waves broke and swam through the troughs towards shore. My instincts told me to come about with the wind and make a tack to bring him back aboard. But I also knew that if I came about this close to shore, we were bound to capsize. In these shallow waters with the heavy surf, we would be pulverized. I held course. We watched the man swim as long as we could while exchanging glances between the approaching shore and the vanishing Good Samaritan.

With shore bearing down on us and less than one-half mile to go, we had to focus. Our only hope was to match speeds with the incoming surf and ride with the waves. Hopefully the waves would push us far enough up the beach that we could jump to safety and pull the Hobie up and out of the raging surf. As if being pushed by Poseidon himself, the little Hobie caught a wave and surfed high onto the beach. Quickly we grabbed the bow lines and dragged the little Hobie up onto the beach and out of the surf. Collapsing in the sand, we both caught our breath.

Then like a lightning bolt it hit me. I screamed, "The guy!" Leaping to our feet, down the beach we ran. With every breaking wave we looked for signs of our sailing companion. We scoured the beach for the life jacket we had thrown him. We searched up and down the beach. We asked the few people who lived on that stretch of beach if they knew of a man that fit our swimmer's description. No one did.

The next morning I returned to the beach looking for some sign of the little man who had been there in my time of need, yet nothing turned up. For several days I kept an eye on the local paper and listened to the marine radio for reports of missing swimmers during the storm, but none were reported. It just did not make sense, and my only logical conclusion was that he probably was just a retiree camping along the dunes somewhere and just happened to be there when I was ready to give up. To a twenty year old college student, this was very acceptable reasoning.

Little did I know that my relationship with the man on the Hobie Cat that day would keep me focused on an incredible journey if I was just willing to walk and listen.

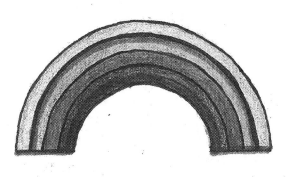

Chapter 2 A Familiar Voice

Rainbow Acres

As a young person, I was a very active lad. My mom raised my sister and me mostly on her own with the help of family. She is a remarkable lady who always put her children first. In the 7th grade when my mom and dad split up, my mom was even more determined to make sure that my sister and I were both a success. She surrounded us with books to read and opportunities for our minds to grow. She kept us involved in church and athletics. Both my sister and I were involved in band and choir. She even arranged a library in our house. As a kid, I was always impressed that we had all those books. Little did I notice that this place I called the library was little more than big planks set up on concrete blocks on an old screened in porch on the front of our house. At any rate, I would go out there and look through the books and pick one up to read and dream about other places and possibilities. My mom was always finding new books to place on the shelves so it was always an adventure to see if my mom had placed anything new on the shelves.

One day while browsing in the library, I noticed a book with a paper jacket on it. A picture of a rainbow arched across its cover and spine. I read the title: <u>Reach for a Rainbow</u>. It looked interesting so I pulled the book off the shelf and read the preface inside the front cover. It was some book about a Baptist preacher and an accident he had while building his ranch. It did not really strike me at the time so I placed it back on the shelf and moved on. I'm not sure what I chose to read that day but what sticks with me is the fact that every time I went to the library after that day I always noticed the book with the rainbow.

Time went by, and I graduated from high school. I was singing and acting by this time with some local success. I had made my plans to go to college and study to receive a Speech Communications and Theater degree along with a teaching certificate to fall back on in case I didn't make it big in the entertainment business. Mom had always said to have a back-up plan! As I was packing for college I wandered out to the library on the porch. I thought I'd take a few of my favorite books with me to reread while in college. As I went through the shelves and pulled a few of my favorites, I heard someone say, "Don't forget the book with the rainbow." As a college bound young know-it-all, I understood that I was just thinking to myself. I pulled it off the shelf and thought I really should read this book. So I threw it in with my things as I went off to face the world.

Time went by at school and things were going very well. I loved the college life, my grades were good, I was singing and dancing in the theater department, I had formed a Christian band called "Light Shine" and we were doing well. Everything seemed to be falling into place. Or so I thought .... It happened on a Friday night. My buddies and I were a little bored with dorm life so we were sitting around playing cards late one night. One of the guys said he needed some milk crates to store his books, and he wondered if anybody had any extras. No one did, but one of the other guys suggested that we just go to the grocery store and get some. In a matter of moments we were loaded into my buddy's van and headed to scope out the local groceries. We found one with stacks of milk crates on the loading dock behind the store. We backed the van right up and began loading. We pulled away with the van full and felt pretty good about finding our prize. We all stopped breathing when flashing lights appeared in front of us and behind us. We were pinned down between several local police cars. As we were handcuffed and each escorted to separate cars, we were all in shock. It was made evident to us that there had been a rash of stolen milk crates, hundreds of them. The milk company that owned the crates was pressing charges. The police were convinced that we had been stealing them regularly, and that they had caught the right people. We were booked and forced to call our parents to bail us out. We showed up for the initial hearing and plead guilty. A sentencing date was set. As I returned to my dorm room it was definitely one of the lowest points in my life. Everything I had worked so hard for seemed to be now disappearing out of my reach. With a felony conviction, I would not be able to obtain a teaching license. The liberal arts college I was attending would most likely not allow us to return to campus the following semester. Everything was falling apart.

My roommate returned home with his parents after we were released so I was alone in my dorm room with nothing to do but think . . . . Studying seemed pointless if I was going to be let go by the college so I laid in my bed, mad at myself and the world.

Then one evening I decided to pack up my stuff and get ready to move home. I had come to the conclusion that "getting out of Dodge" was the best thing I could do (an old saying I had learned from my western novels). As I packed up, of course my hands ran across the book with the rainbow. Then a familiar voice in my head said "READ IT!" So I sat down on my bed and started to read, after all I had been carrying this book around forever. As I began to read, I was captured. I read page after page about a man's dream to make the world a better place. I read about Reverend Showers' own personal setbacks, including the loss of his limbs, while trying to move a building to a ranch he dreamed of building for other abled people. I read about perseverance and pressing forward with God's help. As I finished the book that same night, I closed the cover and I cried. How could I be so weak? Here was a man who could have given up, but instead he found the courage to charge forward and change the world. I was a Christian and had been raised in the Brethren Church. My faith was strong, yet I had not turned to God for help in my current situation. Instead, I was running away. I knelt beside my bed and prayed the only prayer that came into my head, the Serenity Prayer. My mom had hung it above my bed when I was young. I had said that prayer hundreds of times as a child. "God grant me the serenity to accept the things I cannot change, the courage to change the things I can, and the wisdom to know the difference." With that I fell fast asleep.

When I awoke the next morning, I unpacked my things. I was not running from anything. I would stick it out and go where God lead me. I would take the consequence and forge a new path if I had to. I placed the book with the rainbow on my desk as a constant reminder that if a Baptist preacher can go on after losing his arms, I can get through this minor problem of mine.

Two weeks passed, and the four of us who were now called the milk crate gang around campus, had to appear before the judge for sentencing. We were prepared for the worst. The judge handled all four of us at the same time because he told us our sentence would be the same. We were instructed to stand, and the judge started the sentence. He read the statute to us for the felony crime we had been charged with, and we listened. Then he told us he was reducing the charge to a misdemeanor including a trespassing charge. It seemed that a few nights before our sentencing date, the police had arrested the real Milk Crate Gang and had found thousands of stolen crates intended for resale to students at many colleges. The judge informed us that the milk company wanted to drop the charges, yet he thought we should still be charged with something. After all, what we did was still wrong and against the law. We were told to stay clean and never appear before him again. Each one of us paid a $100 dollar fine. We were released. In my opinion, God had given us a reprieve.

As I returned to my dorm room and sat down at my desk, I picked up the book with the rainbow and held it in my hands. "Thank you, Reverend Showers, for giving me the courage to not give up and face the adversity in my life". While this may seem like a very fitting end to the chapter, It is only the beginning of my story and my relationship with a book called Reach For A Rainbow, and a very familiar voice.

I graduated from college and settled into a teaching job. I married my sweetheart, Keli. She has been and always will be a great supporter for my dreams. We bought a small farm near Auburn, Indiana about 3 miles from the school where I taught. We started to remodel that old farm house. Through all these times, the book with the rainbow stayed on my book shelf. It was my reminder to never give up. Keli and I both became involved with the little Brethren church around the section and continued to become more and more involved in the community. My singing career was going well, and I was writing several songs for my first album. Life was good. The little book never got pulled off the shelf, and to be honest, I forgot that it was there.

Then one winter Sunday evening, I was asleep on the living room floor with the IU game on television. My wife Keli came out of the kitchen and said, "Is there supposed to be smoke coming out of that wall by the fireplace in the kitchen?" I ran into the kitchen and found smoke rolling out of the wall. Little did I know that the entire roof of the house was engulfed in flames. The neighbor had already called the fire department. I shouted to Keli to grab the important things while I grabbed a garden hose and tried to save our little country house. Keli came out of the house carrying the family photo album and the cat. Bless her heart! When I had said important things I was thinking more like the filing cabinet and important papers. Ha!

The next thing I knew people were pulling into our driveway. They were entering our house and carrying things out. As the fired rolled up the roof, people were removing our furniture, papers, quilts, food, anything they could lay their hands on. Evidently, the little Brethren Church around the section was having a Sunday evening social when someone said the new couple's house was on fire. They all dropped what they were doing and came to help. It was an amazing story in itself. The following Sunday people started coming up to us and said things like "We've got your kitchen table and chairs. Just let us know when you need them." or "I've got a box of your green beans. Let me know when you are ready to start cooking again." The little Brethren Church members were just keeping our things for us that they had salvaged. One farmer had my wife's hutch that had been given to her by her grandparents. It was simply amazing! That little church was looking out for our every need. About 2 weeks after the fire, the pastor stopped by to see my wife and check how we were doing. We were struggling a little. We had backed a camper loaned by a friend up to our barn. We were trying to live in the camper but it was a trying time. The pastor in his wisdom must have said something to the elders of the church. The very next Sunday a little white-haired widow lady named Anna Ruth came up to us and introduced herself. She went on to explain that since her husband had passed away, her house was just way too big. She informed us that we would be coming home with her after church to get settled in. Since her house was only two miles from our little farm, it would be easy to keep an eye on our livestock and begin to work on our new house. We were in amazement. When we arrived, she showed us around her home and the beautiful 3 bedroom basement we would be calling home. Now how does all this tie in? Anna Ruth also showed us a few boxes some church members had dropped off at her house when she had told them we would be moving in. She told us it was the boxes of things we would probably need, like important papers and such. As I sat down and opened a box to see what was salvaged, what do you suppose I saw? You guessed it. In the box was a little book with a rainbow on the cover. Never give up, Jed . . . . Keep moving forward is what it said to me.

We went on to build a new house. A solid log home, complete with book shelves. We put our lives on track and kept moving forward. The little book with the rainbow continued to be a symbol of hope for me, and a reminder to never give up.

A year or so went by. Keli and I decided it was time to start a family. We were ready to become parents so we threw caution out the window. Yet, after several months we had still not conceived. We consulted our family doctor who ran several tests and found everything to be in order. Keli and I were being very attentive to trying to get pregnant but it just wasn't happening. The months continued to pass. So after a long fall and winter we decided to take a little vacation. March was just around the corner and spring break was coming, so we decided to visit Keli's grandparents in Phoenix, Arizona. We decided to not worry about getting pregnant and just relax. We needed to spend some time not worrying about things. We arrived in Arizona and the weather and everything was great. We played cards, talked and just hung out. Then in the middle of the week, Keli's grandparents decided that we should see some sights. They suggested the Grand Canyon and a little mining town named Jerome. They also wanted to take us to a place called Sedona. We decided to head north for several days. As we got into the car and headed out, my mind began to ramble. I am not a very good rider. I like to drive, but when I am riding, my mind tends to wander. I started to think about having a family, and if Keli and I would ever be able to be parents. We had promised each other not to talk about it on the trip so I didn't say anything. But it was just getting heavier on my mind as we drove north.

Keli's grandparents always liked to take the scenic route. So before long we were off the main road and headed to one of those little towns that are marked with a dot on the map. The scenery was just beautiful. As we drove and talked, the thoughts of not having a family some day to share moments like this kept running through my mind. I just couldn't focus on the trip. I was in agony. Then a familiar voice somewhere inside my head said, "Don't worry about things. Look at the signs." Then as I looked out the window, what sign do you suppose I read? A sign with an arrow that said "RAINBOW ACRES".

My mouth dropped. I yelled "what did that sign say?" Grandpa said he hadn't noticed. I persuaded him to stop and back up. Sure enough, I was right. I told Keli and her grandparents about the book I had about the place listed on the sign. We needed to go see it. They were up for the adventure so we headed down the road to Rainbow Acres.

My heart was racing. I couldn't believe I had just stumbled on to the place were the book with the rainbow came from. How often over the years had I heard a voice giving me wisdom but had chosen to dismiss it as an idle thought? How often had I heard a voice telling me to do something but I had done something different? Now in the middle of a desert, I had heard this voice inside my head once again saying, "Don't worry about things. Look for the signs."

We pulled in that day in March of 1987 and had a great afternoon. A rancher gave us a tour. We spent some time talking to people, and then we were on our way. A sort of peace came over me that was just assuring and for some reason once again I knew that everything would always be ok in my life if I put God first. That night I told Keli that I was finished worrying about what was going to happen to us and our possibilities of having a family. We just had to go with whatever happens. We had to find the serenity to accept the things we could not change!

The rest of the vacation was awesome. The funny thing is, almost 9 months exactly from that day the first of our three children, Austin Lee Freels, was born. It was also only a matter of time before I connected the familiar voice in my head with a familiar face from the past.

Chapter 3 Running on Overload
The Barn Fire

As the smoke cleared and the sheep began to escape the barn, I turned back to the remains of the wooden manger . . . I glanced at the barn door, but he was gone . . . . yet his face and his familiar voice would be forever tied together from this day forward.

7 days earlier

*N*ow I don't need to tell some of you this, but raising a one year old can be a real challenge, especially for someone like me. I was still pushing things to the limit. Thankfully with my teaching job, the farm, and a little canvas company we had started to make minor repairs on things like tents and boat covers, Keli was able to stay home with Austin full time. That being the case, I was sure beyond a shadow of a doubt that Austin was growing up to be the smartest young child ever raised. By the age of one he could talk and walk and what else mattered? Well, yes he could also use the potty by himself, but every time he did he expected an M&M out of the candy jar next to his little chair. Life was pretty good. Keli was seven months along with our second child, and everything seemed to be falling into place. But you know how it goes, just when you get used to hitting fast balls, someone has to go and throw you a curve ball!

These were the days before cellular phones and e-mail. When a call came into school from the outside world, the call actually went directly to the secretary. We didn't have phones in our classrooms so at this point the secretary had three choices. If the call was not especially urgent she would send a message to the teacher with an office runner. If the phone call was important, she would page your room and interrupt your class so that you could call the person back on your break. Or if the call was urgent, she would show up at your door. On this Monday morning, the secretary showed up at my door.

Now when the secretary, Karen, showed up at my door, I knew one of two things was usually happening. Our sheep were out again and running around in someone's yard or something was wrong at home with Keli or Austin. Currently it was winter, and I had the sheep penned up in the barn for the start of the lambing season. I knew it had to be the latter. You couldn't ask for a better secretary because Karen was always calm, cool, and collected. She simply walked in and said, "You need to go call Keli. I'll watch your class." So off to the office I went.

Keli picked up on the first ring, and I asked what was wrong. In her concerned mother voice she explained that Austin was not breathing right. He seemed to be short of breath all the time, and she thought it was getting much worse. I told her to get him bundled up. I would be right there. We only lived three miles from school, and the great thing about working for Dekalb Central is that we were family. If something happened, we covered for each other and did whatever we could to ensure the best education for our students and the best support system for our faculty. When I told the principal that Austin was sick, he simply said, "See ya, let me know what we can do." and out the door I went.

By the time I got home, Keli was in a little bit of a panic. She had called Dr. B's office. The nurse had said to take Austin straight to the emergency room, and Dr. B would meet us there. Sure enough, as we pulled into Dekalb Memorial, Dr. B met us at the door and admitted Austin. Very quickly they decided that his oxygen rate was too low. Dr. B continued to explain that for some reason this meant that Austin's lungs were not converting oxygen into his blood stream properly. Lack of oxygen saturation could lead to serious hypoxia, or an inadequate supply of oxygen to the body. A variety of things could be causing this, and Austin needed to be admitted to an intensive care unit for tests and observations. That would mean moving Austin to a bigger hospital about forty minutes to the south. So back into the car and south we went. When we arrived at the hospital they were expecting us, since Dr. B had called ahead. Austin was quickly placed in ICU. His little bed was placed in an oxygen tent, and we waited.

At this point, plans had to be made on several fronts. I needed to get to a phone. Keli needed rest. Keli's parents lived the closest to this major hospital. They were only ten minutes away. I used my calling card on a hospital phone. Her parents were on their way to pick up Keli. She did not want to leave, but she needed to rest since she was seven months along. We did not want anything to happen to her or the unborn baby. My Mom and Dad would head to the farm to do chores and check for newborn lambs. We had fifty ewes expecting, and in order to have lambs ready for the Easter market, we had started lambing early. So far we had three sets of twins on the ground, and forty seven ewes to go. After doing the chores mom would drive to the hospital and sit with me.

I quickly called the school secretary and explained the situation. I would need to take some time to be at the hospital with Austin. Being a young teacher, I didn't have many sick days. We only received seven sick days each year at that time, and I needed to save some for when the baby was born. With the secretary's help, I decided to teach each morning and take the afternoons off to be at the hospital. She would find a half-day substitute for me.

A quick talk with Keli, and things were in place. I would stay all night at the hospital so she could be at her Mom's to get some rest. In the morning, I would leave the hospital around 6am and head to the farm to check on lambs, and then off to school. My mom would sit with Austin until Keli arrived at the hospital. Keli would take the morning and early afternoon shift while I was at school in the morning and then I would run home to check on the lambs before I came back to the hospital to stay with Austin for the rest of the afternoon and through the night. Then, if necessary, we would repeat it all over again.

Morning one was a blur. I had slept in the chair next to Austin's little tent while holding his hand. His oxygen rate was still too low. Mom relieved me, and I headed to the farm. There were two sets of newborn twins to pen up and make sure they were nursing. Then a quick shower and off to school. Lesson plans were made out for the next three days. At noon it was back to the farm. No new lambs had arrived so I did a quick check of water and feed. Back to the house for a quick shower and phone call to Keli at the hospital. There was no change in Austin's condition. So I went back to the hospital. Keli and I spent some time catching up at Austin's bedside. Then off to her Mom's she went to get some rest. My worries were not only for Austin, but for Keli and the baby as well.

Morning two progressed as a mirror image of day one with the exception that lambs were dropping one right after another. Old Doc Ginther used to tell me that was a sign of a storm on the way. He was right!

On morning three, the storm was upon us, slippery roads, snow to plow, more lambs, but most important and disheartening, no change in Austin's condition. The doctors were not sure. "Could be viral" . . . . "May just have to run its course" . . . . "We'll need to run some more tests". My poor little one year old was poked some more and tested some more and kept right on living in his little tent. I made the trip home and followed the same routine.

Morning four started like the rest except Mom was running a little late because of the roads. I had not slept much so I went down to the cafeteria to get a cup of coffee to keep me awake on the drive home. When I arrived home, I noticed that the barn doors had blown open and that snow had drifted into the lambing area. New lambs had been born, and all my nursing pens were full. Quickly, I closed the barn doors and climbed the ladder to the loft. Our lambing barn was a big old bank barn built in the late 1800's. We could store twelve hundred bales of straw and two thousand bales of hay with room for wagons in the middle. I threw down six bales of straw for new bedding and three bales of hay for feed. I quickly spread the straw around the lambing area and divided the hay between the four wooden mangers. I moved some energetic three-day-old lambs and their mothers out of the nursing pens to make room for the newborns. I made a quick check on the water and dashed for the house since I was running behind. School went quickly. I went home to check the barn and found that all was in order. Back to the hospital I went.

Morning five brought no change in Austin's condition. As a matter of fact, his rate seemed to be going even lower. I was tired. I was frustrated. I was scared. I wanted my little boy to be better, and I wanted us all to be home. As I made the forty minute drive home, I realized how drained my energy was yet my day was just starting. I needed to sleep. I needed to see some sign of hope that the end was near. I needed Austin to get better. I just did not know how much more of this routine I could take. "Lord," I prayed, "I just cannot take anymore." Thankfully, it was Saturday. Without school, after chores I planned to take a quick morning nap before heading back to the hospital. Little did I know . . . .

As I crested the small hill in the road and approached the last quarter mile to the farm, I was greeted by a strange sight. There seemed to be a winter fog around the farm. That did happen occasionally in Indiana. When the weather turned warm quickly, the melting snow could cause fog. Trouble was, I did not think it had warmed up at all. As I turned into the farm drive, I noticed the lights on in the lambing barn and the small entry door standing open. The fog seemed to be hanging around the lambing barn. As I drove down the drive to the massive structure, a fear rocked me to my very core. This was not fog, it was smoke. The smoke was not hanging around the barn, it was coming from the barn!

Leaping from my truck, I dashed for the barn. Bursting through the open door, I could see the sheep huddled against the back wall. I froze in terror. I was not sure what to do. If I opened the main barn doors it would let more air in and the entire place could burst into flames. Suddenly, a man grabbed me by the shoulders. A man I did not know, but a man I recognized. A man who was a stranger, but at the same time there was something familiar about him. I did not know him, yet I knew I could trust him. "It will be fine, the fire's out. Get the sheep to safety." he said. That voice, his face. I must know this man from somewhere . . . . "Go on!" he commanded. I ran across the barn floor and threw open the double doors. Once Tammy, my lead sheep, left the barn the other sheep would all follow, and they did. I ran to the nursing pens and opened the gates so that the newborn lambs and mothers could escape to fresh air. I glanced at the barn floor where there used to be a wooden manger. It was gone. A quick look to the door, but he was also gone.

With the smoke clearing and the sheep safely in the side paddock, I surveyed what had just happened. There, where a wooden manger had once stood, was a pile of ashes and nails. Around the ashes were a worn and watered down path and a five gallon bucket about one-forth of the way full of water. It appeared that the newborn lambs had pulled out an electric water heating element that was in a watering trough near the wooden manger. The heating elements were the kind that have a little float on them so that they stay on the surface of the water as the level in the water tank changes. Below the float is an electric element on a thermostat that can get very hot if not submersed. With all the fresh straw put down the previous day, it didn't take long for the fire to start and spread to the manger. The ceiling in the lower level of the barn was simple one hundred year old wooden planks and above the manager were fifteen hundred bales of alfalfa for winter feed. The only thing that separated the burning manger and the second story hay mow was a two inch wooden floor. Yet someone walking in circles had kept the fire in check and prevented it from spreading. It appeared that water had been splashed on the ceiling to keep it from igniting. The straw around the manager was damp. You could tell someone had been wetting down the straw to keep it from bursting into flames and engulfing the entire barn. But who would have been here to do this? Who kept this fire in check? Who was responsible for saving the sheep, the barn, and my spirit? My thoughts went to the face of the man standing in the door when I arrived. At first I thought it was Roy, the neighbor who lived on the farm across the road or maybe Bob from next door? But I was sure it was not Roy or Bob. I would have recognized them. It had to be someone that I knew, someone that I trusted. It was someone that was looking out for me, but who? My brain raced as I tried to put the voice and the face together. The answer was there locked away in my memories someplace. "Who was it?" I thought. "Think" I screamed inside! Then it hit me. Like a flash fire from my past, it burned a picture for me to see, a picture so vivid and a memory so clear that it rocked me to my very soul. My knees felt weak and the humbleness of the moment began to overtake me. Slowly I emptied the water bucket, turned it over, sat down and cried.

The voice I had heard as I walked into the barn was the same voice that I had always heard inside my head. The face I had seen was the same face I had pulled onto the capsized Hobie Cat so many years ago. They were one and the same. Now in my time of need, a time when someone knew that I could take no more on this particular morning, I put two and two together and realized that a guardian angel was walking with me. Not just today, but every day. I cried some more. "Lord, what have I ever done to deserve your everlasting grace and your daily help?" Moments passed into minutes, and I don't know how long I sat there but I was moved from my trance by a warm muzzle against my cheek. It was Tammy, my lead sheep. Keli and I had raised her from a baby many years ago, she was our first bottle fed lamb. She bahed and looked back out the door. I followed her gaze to see a lamb being born in the snow. It was time to get back to business.

The events had thwarted my plans for a morning nap. As I drove back to the hospital, my adrenaline peaked. My mind was racing a mile a minute with my new revelation. A guardian angel . . . why me? How do I tell anyone? Who would believe me anyway? What do I call him? The only guardian angel I know is Clarence from *"It's a Wonderful Life"*. That's it, I'll call him Clarence! "Clarence," I called "Thank you!"

As I arrived at the hospital and walked back to Austin's unit, I noticed all the families in different rooms. Each had a set of problems of their own, and I realized I was not alone. Each of these families had worries and fears just like I did. Each one of them was hoping for a speedy recovery or a miracle for a loved one. I began to get angry. "Clarence, why will you save my sheep but not my child?" Yet inside I knew that I had no right to question the grace that had been bestowed upon me.

As I approached the nurse's station, I paused to gather myself before I walked into Austin's room. I knew by this point on a Saturday the room would be filled with Keli and family. As I stood there, I glanced at the bulletin board. It was filled with letters from parents who had been standing in my shoes before. The letters spoke of fabulous nurses and doctors. They told stories of recoveries and of losses, but each one conveyed a sense that a sick child could be in no finer place. Then a voice from behind me somewhere said "He'll be fine. Go see Keli." A smile twisted its way up my tired face, and I simply said to myself, "Thanks, Clarence."

As I walked into the room, Keli greeted me with a smile and said, "His oxygen levels are up, he's getting better." And from eyes that I thought had no more moisture left, the tears flowed.

A few days later, Austin was released from the hospital, and we were back at home in the cabin. He would be on a breathing machine for a while for three treatments a day but he would be fine and should recover completely.

Two months later on March 1st, our baby daughter, Carrie, was born. A child that would change our lives forever.

Chapter 4 Rewriting the Future

A Swinging Floor

With a chainsaw running in my hand and my dad's crane from Freels' Machine Works idling near the barn, I was hard at work.

Our family was growing and the cabin that Keli and I had built a few years earlier seemed to be getting smaller. Keli and I slept in the loft and Austin and Carrie shared the downstairs bedroom. The common area was filled with school things, farm things and kid things. We simply needed more room.

So I had this wild idea. A buddy of mine had mentioned that they were going to tear down one of their bank barns on a property they owned about five miles to the north of our farm. I asked if he would mind if I tore it down for him. I would do it for no charge as long as I could keep the material I salvaged from the barn. It was a huge barn, one of the largest in our area. It was fifty feet wide by one hundred feet long. The barn was three stories tall and had been built, as most of the barns in our area, with a post and beam construction. The lumber was a mixture of oak, poplar and hickory, all of which was over one hundred years old. After I had salvaged the usable material, I would leave the rest in a disposal pile for my friend. The deal was sealed with the shake of a hand, and my wild idea was put into motion.

My plan was to dismantle the barn, and with the exception of the roof, move it to our place. I would pour new foundations and floors and attach the barn to the cabin. The rebuilt structure would be on a much smaller scale than the original barn but still large enough to fit our needs. Then using field stone from our surrounding fields, I would face the entire structure with field stones. When I was finished we would have a combination log and stone house almost triple the size of the original cabin. So with little money but lots of enthusiasm, I started on the job.

The summer was going fast, yet each day I made progress. Early in the summer I had started with the siding on the big old structure. The big old barn had last been painted white, but that had been long ago. Over the years, the rain and sun had beat on the old barn. The siding had weathered and the color was now a combination of the browns, reds and whites that had been used over the years. Using a big flat bar and a sledge hammer, I carefully removed each piece of siding. This was to be used for interior walls in the new structure.

Then I started to dismantle the lofts which I planned to reconstruct to provide bedrooms, a library and office area. These hay lofts had been constructed out of solid oak beams which had no doubt been harvested from the surrounding area. Each beam was pinned together with wooden pegs that had been hand carved to fit the holes that had been carefully drilled in the logs. Some of the support beams stretched over forty feet. I carefully removed the pins and lifted the beams out of the barn and I tried to imagine the huge trees that were harvested to provide such magnificent wooden beams. Once reassembled, they would symbolize the mighty strength once held by the giant trees from which they had been harvested.

Next was the job of removing the main barn floor. On this particular day in July that is what I was doing. I planned to reuse the floor as it was. The flooring would also be used to deck the new lofts and bedrooms. Some of the flooring would be fashioned into stairs which would replace ladders originally used in the barn. The remainder of the old floor boards would be made into shelves and cabinets.

Today as I worked, the task was not simple. I knew as I removed floor boards that the structure would continue to become weaker. I had already removed all the exterior siding and all the interior lofts. However, the roof remained. The danger in this dismantle process was that eventually the structure would become weak enough and would not be able to support the roof. The overall goal was to eventually get to a point so that just a few key beams would need to be pulled. This would allow the roof to collapse to the ground. Once the barn had collapsed, it would be more difficult to salvage undamaged lumber. So I was trying to get everything out that I could before I collapsed the barn.

In the process of removing the floor boards, I was also removing the beams which supported the floor. I would take my chain saw and cut sections of the old barn floor loose. Then using the crane, I would lift each section out through the siding less walls into the field beside the barn. At this point I would remove the floor boards from the old beams. After dismantling the section I would load the used lumber on an old school bus that my Dad had converted into a big flat bed truck. It still looked like a school bus from the front, but he had shortened the seating area to only two seats. The rest of the bus was left open to haul things like hay and during this particular summer, lots of barn parts.

The day was going fairly smoothly, and I had about half a load on the old bus when Keli arrived with the two kids to bring me lunch. After shutting everything down, we found a place to sit and eat. Keli was very patient with my project, but she was not overly impressed. All of our friends seemed to be building new homes or moving into different houses as their families grew. Our cute little cabin just seemed to be getting more and more surrounded with piles of debris. There were piles of doors and piles of siding in various lengths. There were piles of flooring sorted by thickness and piles of beams sorted by size. There were piles of stones and reinforcing rod to build foundations. There were piles of bricks, barn tracks, and windows. All were pieces of the puzzle I saw in my head. The problem was that Keli could not quite see the picture in my head. All she saw was the mess building up outside. But she had faith that I had a plan and was supportive every step of the way. This brings us back to lunch on that hot July day.

We had finished eating, and Keli was feeding the baby. Carrie was now four months old and starting to really get some personality. She would laugh and giggle and warm our hearts with her smile. Austin and I were playing in the field. As Keli finished feeding Carrie, I told him that Daddy needed to go back to work so he needed to go sit with mom. I would wait until Keli and the kids were gone before starting things up again for safety reasons so I walked out into the partially dismantled structure. Earlier I had seen a straw deposit beneath the floor on top of a supporting beam. I had not wanted to run the chain saw through it for fear of hitting something and dulling the chain. So I walked out on the beam to check the straw and shake it loose. To my surprise, down deep in the straw, the barn swallows had built a mud nest. Staring up at me were five little barn swallows. This was unusual because normally barn swallows build their mud nests in the open on the side of a beam or some part of the open structure. Then it occurred to me that the straw around and covering the nest must have fallen there as part of the barn dismantling process. Then, without thinking, I spoke those words that are forever burned in my consciousness. "Keli, you should see these baby birds."

As I heard the floor squeak, I looked up just in time to see Keli walking towards me. Then the barn floor that I had earlier cut and made ready for removal, swung like a trap door allowing Keli, with Carrie in her arms to plummet to the concrete floor in the lower level of the big old barn.

Instantly and without thinking, I raced to the hole that they had fallen through. As I peered down into the lower level, I saw Keli and Carrie lying motionless on the floor. My heart pounded. I grabbed the beam and swung myself into the lower level next to Keli and Carrie. They were covered in dust and straw and I saw no movement. Carrie was lying on Keli's stomach. Keli's arms had not moved to brace her. They were still wrapped around her child in the ultimate sign of a mother's love and protection. Quickly I picked up Carrie. Her mouth was full of debris, but as I cleared it she gagged, coughed, and then cried. I turned to Keli with Carrie in my arms and screamed, "Keli, are you OK?" No response. My CPR training kicked in and quickly I put two fingers on the side of Keli's neck. She had a pulse! Gently I shook her shoulder saying, "Keli, can you hear me?" She moaned slightly and said "What happened? Where's Carrie?" "Right here. Everything is fine, "I replied. But I knew that things were not fine. Carrie was crying uncontrollably, and the blood was starting to pool behind Keli's head. Compression and pressure I thought. Quickly and carefully while holding Carrie, I took off the old tank top I was wearing and placed it behind Keli's head. "I need to get you guys to the hospital. Can you move?" I asked. "I'm not sure," Keli responded. "Stay here and don't move." I directed "I'm taking Carrie with me. I'm going to drive your car around behind the barn and get you loaded if you can move. Otherwise, I am calling an ambulance." Keli smiled back at me in understanding.

Then a voice so tender, soft, and young floated down to my ears from above. "Daddy, can I come down?" Looking up, I saw little Austin standing on the edge of the partially collapsed barn floor. His weight was not enough to swing it free, but he was on the edge all the same. I panicked. Do I put Carrie down and get ready to catch him? Do I drag Keli out from under the teetering floor where Austin was standing? God, what do I do?

At that moment from somewhere behind me or somewhere in my head, I heard that voice say, "Tell him to get on the bus." It was Clarence. So in the most loving and gentle voice I could muster under the circumstances I said, "Austin, I need you to go sit on the bus until I come to get you. Daddy loves you!" With a simple 18 month old reply, "Ok," he turned and walked away.

With Carrie in my arms, I raced for the car. Quickly I placed her in the car seat and jumped behind the wheel. I reached for the ignition . . . no keys! Keli! I thought, like the great mom that she always was, she routinely removed the keys from the ignition so that Austin would not accidently start the car. Back to the barn I raced. As I entered, I noticed that Keli had rolled over to her side. That is a good sign I thought. She can move. "Keli, I need the keys!" I stated. "In my pocket," was her weak reply. Grabbing the keys, back to the car I ran. Carrie was crying. I started the engine and drove around the barn. Racing back to Keli, I thought through my options. I knew that a fall victim should never be moved unless they can do it on their own for fear of complicating the injury. I had to make a choice. No Phone. No close neighbors. Two people that needed to get to the hospital. I prayed "Lord, let her be alright." I cradled Keli in my arms and carried her to the car.

With Keli and Carrie now loaded, I jumped behind the wheel and drove around the barn and up the old drive. "But wait . . . . AUSTIN!" Throwing the car in reverse, I backed up the drive to the bus. As I ran around the bus, I heard his voice singing one of our favorite little songs, "The wheels on the bus go round and round, round and round, round and round." Picking him up off the bus steps where he was sitting, I asked "Are you ok, Buddy?" He smiled and said "We've been fine, Daddy." And he hugged me! I knew beyond the shadow of a doubt that Clarence had been sitting right there beside him the entire time.

Doc B's office was connected to the hospital so for some odd reason that is were I headed. As I burst into the office with

Carrie in my arms, I stated, "Darcy. Keli and Carrie have been in an accident." Darcy was Doc's lead nurse and she had watched our kids grow. She said, "Give me the baby, can you get Keli in here?" "I think so," I responded, and out the door I went. When I returned with Keli in my arms and Austin close behind, the receptionist directed me to the back examining room. Doc B was already cleaning Carrie, and Darcy helped me get Keli up on the table. Keli was doing better and seemed to be very aware of what was happening. Doc checked her vitals and said we needed to get Keli and Carrie over to the Emergency Room. He was always very thorough and checked everything.

I asked to use the phone and called my mom. Within minutes mom had called the people that needed to know and shortly our support systems were in place. We were in good hands.

Keli was admitted to the hospital. Her spleen was damaged and she had lacerations to her head and scalp that required staples. She was battered and bruised but she would be OK.

Carrie finally stopped crying and was to be sent home with me. It would not be until almost five years later that we would start to understand the true extent of Carrie's injuries. Injuries that would leave her handicapped for the rest of her life. Injuries that would impact our entire family both immediate and extended, forever. Injuries that would through adversity, strengthen and enrich our family.

I was learning that things do not always turn out the way I thought they should. I was realizing that bad things do happen to good people. I was starting to understand that there are no guarantees in life, but without a doubt we are in control. We can choose to worry about the future or languish in the past. At this point on the journey I had no idea what was in store for me, but I was learning that I had to look for the good in each and every situation, even if that situation had my own life hanging in the balance.

Chapter 5 Check In or Check Out

The Crash

Our little farm was quite the place for kids to grow up. We had all sorts of animals around. Cats and dogs that Keli had rescued from the shelter or along the road, made our porches and patios look like the petting station at the zoo.

Cows and calves were lazily eating at the hay mangers. Horses were grazing in the pastures along side the mother sheep and their lambs. There were rabbits for 4H because, heaven forbid, we could never eat one.

We had goats because the auctioneers just happened to have three that day at the livestock sale. With Keli and the three kids sitting in the front row so they could see all the animals, it was just too easy for her to hold up my number. They (the goats) rode home in a big cardboard box in the back of the car!

Fresh eggs were gathered by the kids from the hen house each day. If they made it to the house uncracked, they would be cleaned and packaged to be sold to the local neighbors for fifty cents a dozen. When the 'egg cup' as we called it, contained enough money, our youngest son Cody (who had arrived in the family about a year and a half after Carrie) would announce it was time for a Blue Moon run. Off to the car we would go, headed to our favorite corner ice cream stand.

As the farm continued to grow, so did the expenses. I'm not one to complain, but each month when I would get the veterinary bills it seemed the most expensive creatures on the farm were always the cats. There was always one cat sick with something, but we made sure they received the treatment they needed. After all, Keli would not have it any other way.

To offset these farm expenses, I picked up some assorted farming jobs. We custom baled hay and straw. We did some field work and pasture mowing. As our farm grew, so did our machinery needs so I was always looking for the right piece of equipment at just the right price.

So it happens that on the Friday after Thanksgiving, I had made arrangements to look at a new tractor near the Kokomo area. Now when I say "new", I mean new to me. I was always explaining that to my wife, Keli. After all, why pay the new price if we can find a piece of equipment for half the price that will still get the job done. Kokomo was about a two hour drive from home, but it sounded like a good piece of equipment. The tractor was a used John Deere 4020 with a cab. The only owner was retiring from farming, and it sounded like he had taken very good care of the tractor. I thought it was worth a look, so I made the arrangements.

Normally I would just jump in my truck and take off, but on this particular Friday that was not the case. My buddy, Xen, who was always helping me out on the farm needed to borrow my truck that day so we decided to switch vehicles for the day. I would just drive his car so he could use my truck for the day. We met early before the sun was up to get an early start to our day. I wanted to get to Kokomo and back before noon, and Xen wanted to get his things moved early that morning also. We switched keys and both took off to take care of our separate plans.

Xen had just purchased a minivan so when I jumped in it felt very different than my truck. I adjusted the mirrors, moved the seat, turned on the lights, buckled up and started the engine. The minivan was not what I would usually drive to go check out a piece of equipment but it would work.

I turned right out of the driveway and started down a very familiar road, one that I had driven hundreds of times. As I cruised down the road, I was trying to figure out what all these buttons on the dash were. The instrument panel in this minivan was definitely more sophisticated than my old truck. I just wanted to get the radio on and tuned to a station I could listen to along the way. Finally I figured out that you push the little button to turn it on, not twist it like the one in my truck. The next challenge was going to be finding the country station that I liked. As I glanced at the frequency numbers on the radio, I felt the front tires go bump. As I looked up, I realized that which radio station was playing no longer mattered.

I was less than five miles from home. I was on a road that I had travelled hundreds of times back and forth to my parents' house. Yet I had totally forgotten about the 90 degree turn in the road south of Custer Grain.

As the front tires hit the side ditch, I slammed on the brakes but it was too late. The brakes could not stop the 45 mph moving minivan in a split second and that was all the time I had. The minivan shot off the road like a rollercoaster off its track. I had no control. In the blink of an eye, I slammed head on into a tree just off the road. The windshield exploded from the frame, the hood was ripped from the latch and crinkled like a sheet of paper. The dashboard seemed to be folding like modeling clay. Then the engine was twisted from its mounts and shoved backwards, driving the steering column directly at me. There was no airbag deployment. That technology would be on next year's model, but that did not help me now. The steering wheel crashed into my chest, and I slumped over the wheel.

That was the end. There were no flashing lights or scenes from my life. I just stopped living. It was not that my eyes were closed, I just could no longer see. It seemed like my brain was still working, but it was not attached to anything. I could feel the loss of functions and awareness slipping away. This was the end. I had no thoughts, no vision, just an understanding that things were over, and I could do nothing about it. It seemed like I could hear things like the hissing of steam and the still falling pieces of glass from the windows around me, but the sounds meant nothing to me. I could feel the blood running down my face but it didn't matter, it had no effect. I knew that it was time to let go. It was over.

Then a hand came from somewhere, not a hand reaching out to guide me home like we all hope for. But a hand that pushed its way between the steering wheel and my chest, a hand that shoved me with a mighty force back into the seat away from the steering column. Next a voice, a voice I knew and had come to love, bellowed in my mind "LOOK AT ME!" I somehow opened my eyes and there in front of me in someone's hand was the picture from my wallet of my three children Austin, Carrie, and Cody. "IT'S JUST NOT TIME!" the voice thundered. As my gaze followed the outstretched arm that was attached to the hand holding the picture, my vision came into focus on a very familiar face. It was Clarence. He had come to be with me in the end. At least that's what I thought. But he hadn't. He had come to shove me farther down this sacred journey. He had come to make sure I didn't quit. He had come to give me courage. Courage to change the things I can. "YOU NEED TO DRAG YOURSELF OUT OF THIS CAR AND CRAWL TO THAT LIGHT!" he instructed with authority as he pointed. So that is what I did.

I looked at his finger and then in the direction he was pointing. I could vaguely see what seemed to be a distant light in the darkness. Feeling started to come back into my limbs and my chest, feelings of excruciating pain. I couldn't move, but I had to. I reached up and grabbed the door jam through the jagged glass and pulled myself from behind the wheel. Like a rag doll, I fell from the window to the ground and started crawling to the light. As the light grew closer, it also seemed to be getting dimmer. My legs were working and my arms moved, but my entire body was burning with pain. "Pain is a teacher" a wise person once told me. I told myself that now. I screamed to myself "I know you are hurting. I know you are failing. But just keep moving." I focused all my energy to my arms and legs and through the pain I could feel them getting stronger as they carried my torn body and soul. I crawled closer and closer to the light. Finally a step appeared; I dragged myself up onto a front porch. The door was cracked, and I saw a small female face peering out from behind a small crack in a chained door. "Call an amb . . . ." was the last thing I remembered.

At some point I came to for a moment in the emergency room and saw my wife, Keli, and my Mom and Dad standing in the room. At that point I knew I was alive.

The next morning when I woke up, I had been admitted to a regular room. The IV was flowing, oxygen was running, vitals were beeping, but surprisingly enough I had no casts. The only major bandage I had was on my head along with a few minor ones on various extremities. I tried to move . . . mistake. "I think I'll just lie here," I said to myself.

My first visitor was Doc B. Just by chance he had been working in the emergency room when they brought me in. Now he was making morning rounds. As he sat down on the edge of the bed he said, "Good morning, how are you feeling?" "Great" I tried to reply. As I let go a little laugh, my chest felt like an explosion went off inside. "Yea, that's going to hurt for awhile." Doc. B said. "You're lucky to be alive" he told me "Your x-ray shows that your sternum is broken in two places and your ribs crushed on both sides." he paused. Then he added, "99% of all people who have those kinds of breaks from a head-on collision, die on impact. I guess yesterday you were the one percent!" He checked me over and said he would be back later to check on me and that I should get some rest. I tried, but I did not feel like resting. My mind was now running a mile a minute over the events that had just happened. I had been given a second chance, no a third chance, no who knows how many chances? The bottom line is that I had been given another chance! A chance at what, I wasn't sure but lying in that hospital bed at that very moment I prayed.

"Thank You God . . . Thank you for Clarence."

Keli arrived at my room shortly after Doc B had left. Mom had just taken her downstairs to get a bite to eat. When she entered the room, we both started to cry. She tried to give me a hug . . . mistake that too would have to wait. She and mom reviewed the happenings of the last twenty-four hours which I could not remember. Keli said that I had a lot to be thankful for.

I guess the lady who owned the porch I crawled to told the paramedics that she had accidentally left her porch light on. When she heard the crash, she figured some drunk on his way home with an early morning hangover had missed the curve again. She did not unchain the door until the paramedics arrived because you just never know. I was thankful she did dial 911.

The paramedics on call were friends of mine. This was a good thing because I never carried my billfold in my pocket. I cannot stand to sit on it, so I always throw it in the seat beside me. If other paramedics would have been on duty, no one would have known who I was, especially since I was driving someone else's car. I was thankful the paramedics knew me because they called the sheriff's office which sent an officer straight out to the house to tell Keli. She was at the hospital when I arrived.

Keli said that even though Doc B. had told the sheriff's department that this accident did not involve alcohol or drugs, they had insisted on running drug tests on my blood to make sure. I was thankful for that since it all came back negative. I was glad they do their job thoroughly.

Pastor Don from the little Brethren Church we attended had been at the hospital most of the day with family. He had started the prayer chain. I was thankful that I was being lifted up by so many positive souls in prayer.

Keli said our family as always had been right there. I was thankful that our extended families were close so that we could not only share in the joys of everyday life, but also be there to support each other in times of need.

Principal Tom had stopped in to see how I was doing and to assure me that I did not need to worry about school. I was thankful to work for a school community who treated each other like family.

Friends had been calling and coming by already to see what they could do. During one visit by friends my buddy Tim must have noticed that our wood pile was low. Wood was our only source of heat for the winter. The very next Saturday twenty-five people arrived at the farm. They split and cut twenty loads of wood for us to use through the winter. I was thankful for close friends.

But Keli said what I should be most thankful for was to be alive. She was right.

Keli and Mom left to go see the kids, and as I laid there in bed I thought, "I am thankful, thankful to be on a journey." a journey with a final destination that had been postponed again. A journey that for some reason I just needed to keep on walking. As I stared at the ceiling of my quiet hospital room, I began to question. Why do some of us get second chances? Why is it that this guardian angel I had named Clarence keeps coming to me in my times of need? A thought popped into my head, I wish there was some yellow book with black trim entitled *Guardian Angels for Dummies!* I know there would be an entire chapter in there about me. I wanted to believe that there must be some Devine purpose for my Guardian Angel, but I was clueless. Little did I know that some of the greatest moments for my faith to grow were yet to come!

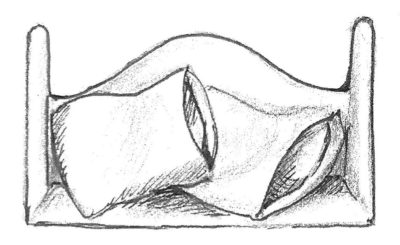

Chapter 6 Looking for Simple Signs.

Bed Time Songs

After the crash, I started to talk more openly with the kids and my close friends about my relationship with Clarence.

I started sharing his story and my journey at the campfires and concerts that I would give. Of course some people were stirred and compelled to share similar stories. People started coming up to me and telling about times when they had heard a voice. They would share about times when something miraculous had happened in their life. They started to share stories about moments in their own lives when they felt that someone else had been there for them.

Some people would share stories about living Angels, people who walk beside us as shepherds, people who are put into our lives for a reason. I started to realize that the scope of having a guardian angel was huge. The fact that they came in so many different ways and forms was inspiring. I started to understand that it was not just me but that in some way, shape, or form, we all had someone looking out for us.

The problem was that with all this positive movement and understanding that there just had to be something greater, I had not noticed the nonbelievers. That fact that somehow everything and everyone is connected was not something that everyone believed in.

While I was busy sharing the positive side of my story, there were those who doubted me. They started asking questions like "Why you?" and "Why didn't God send me an Angel in my time of need?" I didn't have the answers for them. When I would give a concert or share around a campfire, I could see them thinking, "This guy is totally loony." It was during this time of my openness that I began to doubt myself. I started to question if it was right to share something that others could not see. I was not sure if it made sense to reveal with others the relationship that I developed with the spirit that walked with me. Maybe by revealing my relationship with Clarence, I was actually helping people lose faith.

Maybe I shouldn't be sharing my story with people. Maybe a relationship with a guardian is supposed to be a sacred and private matter. Maybe it is intended only to be understood by the people involved.

I began to loose my zest for telling my story. I found myself beginning to doubt what I knew was true. Should I continue to share this sacred journey or not?

Then on one unsuspecting night when I wasn't looking at all, I was given part of the answer.

In our house, one of the biggest challenges was always getting three energetic kids to go to bed. Bed time was 8:00 sharp each night and over the years we had developed a system that worked. I realized early on that bed time had to be something the kids looked forward to or what was the point. Lecturing three little children about the importance of sleep and its overall impact on their health could not compete with The Cartoon Network. In reality, our kids watched very little TV. Mainly because Keli had placed a huge emphasis on their early education and what could have been TV time was usually reading time. So each night around 7:30, Keli or I would make some popcorn. At this point the kids knew that if they wanted popcorn they had to have their pajamas on, teeth brushed, and be ready for bed. Then we would all sit down on the couch to read.

We would read each of their favorites, which would change as they became older. We would read farm books and sports books, silly books and sad books. We would find something new that we thought would challenge their young minds. Sometimes we read books that correlated with the current seasons and sometimes we just read whatever was on top. As they got older and became avid readers themselves, we started in on chapter books and sometimes everyone would take a turn reading a page to each other.

As evolutionary as story time was, one thing remained consistent over the years. As the clock would near 8 o'clock, Keli or I would say those inevitable words "Just one more story." As the story would end it was hug time and a love you for mom, and three little sets of eyes focused on Dad because they knew the race was about to be on. With anticipation they would listen as I announced where the finish line would be. "It's . . . . A . . . . Race . . . . to Cody's Bed!" And away we went.

This was an all out race with the winner receiving satisfaction that they were the fastest person of the day. Now on occasions I will have to admit I won just to boost my own self-esteem. Other times I had to run interference so that the boys didn't win all the time. Sometimes I just let them elbow it out around each corner and up each stair to see who really was going to be first. The finish line would always end up a pile on somebody's bed with the winner getting to pick the first bedtime song. Sometimes depending on where we raced to I would have my guitar there by the bed, other times we would sing without it.

On this particular night Carrie won so we all knew we would be starting with <u>Oh Mr. Moon</u>. After all, one thing you learn early on living with a handicapped child is that you do not mess with their routine =). Austin picked second, and for the life of me I can't find in my rusty old filing cabinet of a brain which song he picked, probably <u>This Little Light of Mine</u>. Then it was Cody's turn. Cody usually thought hard about his pick. He never wanted it to be just any old song. It either had to be fun or have some kind of meaning. Tonight for some reason he chose <u>Angels Watching over Me</u>. I picked the Key of G on my guitar, and we started in. We sang the verses followed by the chorus each time and as the song ended we always sang the chorus twice at the end. Only tonight as we started the reprise of the chorus, Cody changed it up on us all and sang "All night, all day, Clarence is watching over me my lord, all night all day Clarence is watching over me." From that day forward that's how the song always ended.

As we finished songs, we always said our prayers together and each person prayed for someone and mentioned something they were thankful for. I'm not really sure what the kids prayed for that night, but I remember mine. "Lord, be with all those who are in need tonight, thank you for my family and for Clarence."

Never again would I question if I should share my journey with others. If it was simple enough for a child to understand, then it should be simple enough for us all to understand.

Chapter 7 Letting God Drive

Atlanta

Jeff and I were on our way home from Orlando on a whirlwind 48 hour trip. We had started on Good Friday, driving my truck with the car dolly in tow. The mission . . . To pick up a red '66 Mustang I had found on the internet. We had intended for the trip to be a non stop trip, but I guess plans are made to be changed . . . .

Teenage boys and cars—it's a relationship that evolves with each passing drive and my two sons were no exception to the rule. By the time both had graduated from high school and college, they had collectively put up quite a resume. They had been in the ditch on the way to school and town. They had been sideswiped by a sign. They had rear ended the car in front of them. They had somehow landed in the neighbor's front yard, right next to their porch. They had veered off the road and trimmed other neighbor's trees. As a crowning event, they had been upside down hanging by their seatbelts. Of course these are just the ones that were bad enough to tell Dad about. Ha!

Now you might wonder how a red '66 Mustang plays into this so let me explain. In all of the above mentioned "aggressive driving learning situations" (sounds better than wrecks), the Mustang was only involved with one. It was the car that ended up next to the neighbor's front porch. As a rule, and I know this sounds odd and you are going to laugh, but most of the time my boys were pretty good drivers. They took pretty good care of their vehicles. They bought their own gas and usually got themselves from point A to point B without a problem. Cars and trucks were one of the things that motivated them. That is were the Mustang came in.

When the boys were approaching driving age, I was talking with a buddy of mine who owned a body shop in town. Little did I know at the time how much business we would be doing with him over the next several years! Anyway, he was telling me that his philosophy was to buy his kids a classic car. You could usually buy one cheaper than a good used car, and then his kids had something that was pretty cool to drive. They were easy to work on, and they also had a better resale value when the kids were finished driving them. This made a lot of sense to me so when Austin was approaching driving age we started to look for a classic. I had always wanted a '66 Mustang so I believe I may have had a pretty big influence in the situation. The deal was we would buy a Mustang and as long as Austin kept straight A's on his report card, he cold drive it. During the winter months when the roads were bad, he could drive an old Jeep we had.

Finally, after searching for several months, we found exactly the car we wanted at the price we were willing to pay. Location . . . . Orlando. That's about a 22 hour drive straight through from our little ranch in northern Indiana. We checked around with several transport companies and found out how much they were going to charge to bring the car home. Jeff and I decided to road trip. We made arrangements. We would leave around 2 a.m. on Good Friday morning. The plan was to pick up the Mustang in Orlando at midnight and turn right around and head home. That would put us home around midnight Saturday, and we would be up and around for Easter Sunday the following day.

So we hitched up the car dolly and away we went. The trip was going very smoothly. We had arrived in Orlando and closed the deal right on time. We were loaded and headed home within an hour. We had been switching on and off the driving duties, and it was my turn to drive for a few hours. I would get us out of Florida and then Jeff would take the next hitch. Traffic was pretty light at this time of the morning so driving was smooth. We hit the Florida state line and switched drivers. I needed some rest and Jeff was now wide awake. So back on down the road we headed as I settled in to grab a few hours of sleep.

We were just south of Atlanta, I was sound asleep and Jeff was at the wheel when I heard a familiar voice. It was Clarence and with urgency he said, "WAKE UP!" As his statement jolted me, I found myself in that land of partial sleep. During the fraction of a second, you are awake, but not quite fully conscious. At that moment I heard a very specific clank and Jeff said "What was that?" Jerking to an upright position, I glanced in the rearview mirror and my worst fear was confirmed. The car dolly had come unhooked from the truck.

I looked around. The situation was not good. We were just coming into Atlanta. There was a slight drizzle of rain coating the road and the windshield. There were four lanes of solid traffic in front of us and behind us. We were in a middle lane with a car on the left and a semi on the right. I felt the car dolly jerk against the safety chains; they held. The semi to our right swerved onto the berm as the dolly and the Mustang swung to the right. I hollered, "The trailer is off!" I felt Jeff brake. He was a good driver, and I knew he would do everything he could to get us stopped. Then, like an out of control pendulum on a grandfather clock, the dolly and the Mustang whipped hard to the left. They missed the car beside us which had somehow slowed down enough to avoid the collision. However, the swing had been great enough that as Jeff tried to decelerate the truck, the front left corner of the Mustang collided with the rear bumper of the truck. The sounds of crashing glass and lights and bending sheet metal filled the air. The lane to our left opened up. "I'm going to try to get us off the road." Jeff said. The dolly swung back more violently to the right. The right side of the Mustang shattered against the guardrail. The impact sent the dolly swinging to the left again, and then crashing back to the right. As Jeff tried to get us veered to the side of the road, I felt the truck slip loose from the traction it had with the pavement. Looking to my right, I could see the two foot high guard rail. Beyond the guard rail was a steep embankment that rolled sharply down for what seemed like one hundred feet or more. The truck and trailer were now swinging violently out of control. The high pitched sounds of passenger cars and the roar of big rig air horns filled the air. We were headed for the guardrail. I knew that if we hit the guard rail at this speed, the impact would carry us up and over. Somebody shouted, "HANG ON!" I thought Jeff had said it. He thought I had. We both grabbed the rough ride handles attached to the ceiling and hung on. I shut my eyes and braced for the collision.

The truck lurched. I waited for the sounds of the collision which I knew were to follow. They didn't. The truck slowed abruptly, and I felt the trailer collide with the back of the truck. The dolly seemed to be pushing the truck forward. Then we heard the sounds of tires sliding across wet pavement, followed by the sounds of rattling safety chains. The truck rolled to a stop.

I opened my eyes and looked at Jeff. His hands were still locked, one on the rough ride handle and one on the steering wheel. "How did you do that?" I asked. "It wasn't me, someone else was driving," he replied.

As we gathered ourselves and crawled out the passenger door, we surveyed the damage. The truck and the car dolly with the Mustang still fastened down were sitting perfectly in a parallel line about a foot from the guardrail. Mustang parts littered the highway behind us as cars still swerved to miss the scattered debris. The Mustang was a total loss, but we were alive. We were alive and parked along the interstate right next to what should have been our final guardrail.

After sitting for just a few moments, we started to access the damage. We carefully gathered up as many parts as we could and placed them in the back of the truck. We checked the dolly hitch. It was apparent that the entire hitch had slipped out of the sleeve on the back of the truck. The pin had worked its way out, and the hitch had slipped free. I must have forgotten to place the snap pin into the hitch pin when we left home. Somehow the hitch had remained in place all the way to Atlanta and part of the way home. Amazingly, the hitch that had slipped free was still attached to the car dolly. The car dolly was unscathed and seemed to be in good condition. We only had to move the dolly about two inches to get everything in line to be hooked up again to the truck. Hooking up didn't go quite so smoothly. It seemed that during the swinging the tongue latch on the car dolly had been bent. After we released it to get everything hitched back up, it would not resecure itself. We needed to find an auto parts store for repairs. Using a few things we found in the tool box, we secured the dolly well enough to at least get us off the interstate and into Atlanta.

After finding an auto parts store, we found a parking spot and waited for the store to open. We talked about the last hour and the amazing turn of events. We had numerous questions. How had that pin worked its way out, and what happened to the safety pin that holds it in place? How had the car dolly escaped damage, yet the Mustang was totaled. Who had yelled, "Hang On,"? It had to be Clarence. Jeff and I had talked about Clarence on the trip, and it seemed an obvious solution that not only did he yell "Hang On" but he was probably the one driving also. "How about that," we laughed "A Guardian Angel who can drive." The parts store opened, We bought the necessary items, made the repairs, and headed back to the interstate.

At this point we were a little behind schedule but in no hurry. We continued to discuss the turn of events, and we decided that there was no way that the safety pin could have come out. I must have forgotten to clip it in place. But how had it ridden all the way to Orlando and part of the way home without coming out? Why had it suddenly slipped out right in the worst of all situations? Why had our scheduled been altered just enough to demolish the Mustang and then send us back on our way?

Now we were back on the road with the truck running smoothly but our minds racing a mile a minute. One little slip of a safety pin . . . . there had to be a reason . . . . And sure enough, being behind schedule about two hours is exactly what somebody had in mind.

About forty-five minutes passed and Jeff and I were still running on an adrenaline high. We were taking our time and had settled into a comfortable traffic flow. As I drove, we were talking about how life sometimes deals you a hand you just do not understand. We laughed at the fact that we could have probably bought a wrecked Mustang much closer to home. We talked about our faith and how sometimes you just have to trust in the greater good. We talked about how people must be in charge of their own destinies, but at the same time there has to be an interconnectedness between all things. We were both thankful that the accident had not turned for the worst, and I thanked Clarence for being there once again.

As we drove we both noticed that we seemed to be much more aware of our surroundings. We paid close attention to the passing cars and passengers and the scenery we were passing. It all seemed to be much more detailed to us. Every few seconds we were looking in the rearview mirror to make sure we still had the trailer. We were looking for the slightest thing that we might be able to spot and prevent another accident.

It was during this time while looking at the traffic ahead of us Jeff said, "I think that guy ahead of us just blew a right front tire." As I looked closer at the small pickup truck travelling a full six or seven seconds ahead of us, I also noticed that the truck seemed to be drifting off the road like the tire had blown. Then the simple scene turned into something right out of a modern day Hollywood action film.

The little truck suddenly veered sharply off the road and hit a large concrete drainage culvert. The impact sent the little truck flying through the air end over end. Crashing to the ground, the little truck bounced like a rubber toy being thrown down by a toddler. The momentum then threw the truck sideways, and it started to roll across the grassy embankment. The little truck came to rest upside down. I pulled off the road as fast as I could just past the little upside down truck. Jeff grabbed a first aid kit, and we ran to the truck. The tires were still spinning, steam spewed from the engine. Gasoline was draining from the overturned and smashed fuel tank. As we approached the overturned little truck, we saw the driver hanging upside down by his seat belt. Blood was running down the side of his face and without question he was dead.

We stopped. If we moved too close and the truck exploded, we also would be in danger. At this point there was nothing we could do. We watched, stunned by what we had just seen and then the upside down driver moved a hand. Just a small movement, but it was a movement. I was sure of it. "He's alive" Jeff said. Quickly we went to the truck without thinking. There was no hesitation. We needed to get this man out, and we needed to do it now! I reached up through the broken window to find the seatbelt release. It was rigid with pressure, but with the first press it released. The man fell to the overturned roof of the truck. Quickly, Jeff and I started to drag the man clear of the wreckage. A semi truck driver who had also witnessed the accident arrived and started to spray down the wreck with a fire extinguisher.

Jeff and I quickly turned our attention back to the man. Check for pulse . . . yes. Check respiration . . . . good. Check for blood loss. The blood was coming from a head wound which appeared only to be a severe scalp cut. I applied some pressure with a piece of gauze. Check for compound fractures. His arm seemed wretched in an awkward position, but no compound fracture was evident. The rest of him seemed uninjured. He moaned; a good sign. He tried to set up. Then he started to speak, but we could not understand. He started to speak more rapidly. I could pick up bits and pieces. It was Spanish. I had learned just enough Spanish in school to understand that he wanted something from the truck. He tried to get up but could not. He started talking faster and began crying. I tried to calm him down with what little Spanish I still knew, but he continued to point towards the truck and talk. Then I caught it, his Bible. He wanted his Bible from the truck. Back to the truck Jeff walked and retrieved the man's Bible from the overturned truck. It was a worn and tattered Bible which you could tell was well used. Jeff placed it in the man's hands and the old Spaniard began to weep. "Gracious," he cried "Gracious, Gracious". We sat with the man, consoling him the best we could as we tried to keep him still until help arrived. As he opened his Bible, we saw the pictures of his family taped into the front cover. We saw the worn and tattered pages of a book that had not just been read, but obviously lived, by this man we sat with by the side of the road.

Soon help arrived, and one of the officers spoke fluent Spanish. Paramedics quickly took over and our job was done, but yet we lingered on the edge. We watched as the old man was cared for with more capable hands than ours. As they loaded him into the ambulance, he looked our way and with tears in his eyes and holding his family Bible, he said "Gracious, me amigos". "Thank you, my friends."

We climbed back in the truck and headed home.

Now more than ever I understood the interconnectedness of it all. I could not say that we made a difference in saving this man's life. I could not say that the outcome would have been any different if we had not been there. I could not say for sure that the man's family Bible would have been lost in the ruble and the turmoil of the event. But I did know, without question, that for some reason Jeff and I were supposed to be in that situation at that given time. On that day we needed to sit with that man on the side of the road just as Jesus had done so many years before. In this I learned one of the greatest lessons in life. Life is not about asking why bad things happen! Life is about learning from those moments when they do happen. I learned it is not for us to question why little safety pins are forgotten, but sometimes they just are.

Chapter 8 Understanding Wisdom
Carries Placement

Well . . . at this point I will fast forward a little and skip all of the
ball games and soccer matches. It had been twenty seven years
since that day on Lake Michigan when I first met Clarence
and things had gone pretty well. Keli and I had raised our three
children, and we had been blessed over the years. With lots of
hard work I had two albums under my belt, with several singles
that even had a little air time. I had directed a very successful
theater group for seven-teen years of sold-out performances.
Our business ventures, or should I say adventures, had been
very successful. We continued to live on the ranch, as I called
it, and I had been teaching school for twenty-six years. It is
amazing what can happen when you never give up and have a
little help and faith. Yes faith, faith in a little voice I had heard
from time to time in my head, and a faith I had learned to
have in a man that had been there in my times of need. I had
not seen Clarence in awhile, but I had heard him often. I was
beginning to become a better listener when I prayed. Over the
years as I had walked this sacred journey with Clarence, I had
forgotten about the little book with the rainbow until one day
while sitting at my desk . . . and this is where Carrie's story joins
with Clarence.

I was sitting at my desk one night contemplating my daughter's application for a residential placement for other abled adults at a place called Sharing Meadows. It is a wonderful place started by a priest named Father Blainey. Our daughter, Carrie, is a mentally handicapped adult. She was born just fine like her brothers who are very bright and gifted. At the age of four months, she was involved in that accident in the barn. She damaged the nerve bundle called the Articulating Reactivation System. Instead of being able to multi-process things like most adults, Carrie is very limited. She functions at about a 2nd grade level. She has an IQ depending on the test and day of around seventy. She is a wonderful young lady and the joy of our lives. She tries to take care of herself and does her chores. She is in charge of the rabbits and chickens on the farm. However, she requires 24/7 supervision and will never be able to live on her own. Her Traumatic Brain Injury had left her handicapped for life.

My wife, Keli, gave up her teaching career and stayed at home to raise Carrie. We kept Carrie involved, and all through high school she was active. She was on the girls soccer team, sang in the choir, and participated in 4H for 10 years. In every situation, she found a support system that helped her feel worthy.

When she graduated from high school, we began trying to plan her future. We had always thought that her future would be with us here on the ranch. However people encouraged us to find a place where she could blossom on her own. We had hoped we had found that in a place called Sharing Meadows. But sitting at my desk that night, I was wondering if it was the right choice. I had been dragging my feet about returning her application. I could not help but wonder if she would just be happier here with us. After all, who could possibly take better care of Carrie than Keli and me. I was not sure I could ever trust my child to be in the permanent care of someone else. Sitting at my desk, I started to pray for guidance and a path to take. "Lord, over the years you have been there for me in my times of need. Tonight I ask your guidance in this decision. Help me look at this situation in a realistic way and do what is best for Carrie and her needs, not mine. Lord, you have given me the serenity to accept the things I cannot change in regards to Carrie, and you have given me the courage to change the things I can, but I am not sure I have the wisdom yet to know the difference. I am struggling, and Carrie's future hangs in the balance. I don't know where to turn. Lord, thank you for your grace and your mercy. Amen."

As I finished praying and opened my eyes, I felt the presence of Clarence in the room. I saw him standing across the loft looking at the kids' pictures. Each year Keli had hung 8 x 10 photos on the wall of the walkway, that was the bridge between our bedroom and the loft I used as my office and library. Austin, our first child, was across the top. Carrie had the middle row. Cody, our youngest, was across the bottom. Walking across that loft each day had always made me feel like I was walking through time with each of them. "They're growing up," Clarence said. "I'm not so sure I like that, Clarence," was my reply. "Clarence, I am not sure what to do . . . ." I said. Then I proceeded to tell him my struggle. I told Clarence how I wanted the best for Carrie, but I wasn't sure what that was. I explained that in my heart I could not discern which direction to take. I was confused and afraid for Carrie. As I rambled on, Clarence sat down on the small couch in my office and listened. He was my therapist with open ears and an open heart. As I continued on, it finally occurred to me that everything I was saying he already knew. "Clarence, I'm sorry. Why am I telling you things you already know?" He smiled. I continued, "I just don't know what to do." There was a slight pause and then in a voice so calm and collected, a voice that I had heard so many times when I needed reassurance or guidance, he said "Reach for a rainbow."

I thought for a moment and then realized what he was telling me. I turned and pulled <u>Reach for a Rainbow</u> off the shelf. Staring at the cover, I thought "why does this book keep coming up in my life?" I turned to ask him, but of course, he was gone.

As I held the book and prayed I could hear Clarence's voice giving me guidance "Jed, keep moving forward just like Reverend Showers." I was flooded with revelation. Over the years, the book with the rainbow had become a symbol of never giving up and a personal story of moving forward. But now I started to remember other things. I remembered the happiness of the campers I had visited at Rainbow Acres all those years ago. I remembered the stories of how Reverend Showers was building a place for other abled adults to live and be part of a community. I started to find a peace of mind that Carrie will find a place. She will touch other people with her joy and happiness. I realized that Carrie is a child of God, and as I continued to search for the answers I knew that God had a plan for my daughter, Carrie. Just like the plan he had for Reverend Showers that fateful day on the barn roof. It had been almost thirty-five years since that first day when I saw the book with the rainbow on my mom's homemade book shelf. It had been with me ever since. The book had become a symbol to me that everyone has a purpose. No matter what happens in life, we must keep moving forward to try and make the world a better place.

That night after talking with Clarence I realized in so many ways that God had kept the book with the rainbow in my life to give me the strength to raise a handicapped child. I believe He knew that I needed it to keep my faith strong and to keep me moving forward. I believe He placed Clarence in my life along with the book to keep me walking on a sacred journey. I realized that journey was not just my own, but one that also impacted those whose journey crossed paths with mine. Through Clarence, I was realizing that becoming the hands of God, so that He can work through us, is the most important thing we can learn.

Little did I know that doing God's work would not only bring joy, but also sorrow and pain.

Chapter 9 Singing His Praises

Guitar Sunday

It was about twenty-five minutes after midnight when Keli and I arrived home on this particular Saturday night.

We had been to a show choir event that included our singing and dancing son Cody. It had been a long day. Do not take that the wrong way. It was always very enjoyable to watch the boys perform, and over the span of seven years we had been all around the show choir circuit. From Branson to Orlando and from New York City to Chicago, and just about every stop that show choirs make around the Midwest.

These events were very enjoyable, but they were lengthy. First you had the travel time and accommodations to arrange. Then your group sang during the day at an assigned time in front of a huge crowd and usually a panel of six judges. The goal was to make the night show where you have the opportunity to repeat the entire performance. Next you wait to see which choir will rise to be the grand champion of the event. Finally, after the awards, there was the loading of stage equipment, props and wardrobes to prepare for the trip home or back to a local hotel. Under the direction of a remarkable director, the boys' group, Classic Connection, had never been eliminated before the night show. Hence I say it was usually a long day.

On this particular trip, we were close enough to home that Keli and I decided to drive home after the awards ceremony. It was not often that we were able to do that, so when we could we usually did. It always helped us fell like we still had a little of our weekend left.

Upon arriving home, we did a quick check as we always do. Keli took the dogs out for a quick stretch. I checked the messages that had been left that day. I was just finishing up with my last few messages when Keli came back in from walking the dogs. She then proceeded to walk over to the calendar and flip the page. Keli kept an amazing calendar. She had everything written down months in advance if it affected our busy family. It did not matter if it was a kid event, church event, or community event. It might be a doctor's appointment, a car tune up, or even a note that the farrier was coming that day to trim feet and shoe horses. If it was anything that concerned the Freels' Family schedule, it was on the calendar.

On this night after she turned the page, she glanced my way and said "Oh, by the way, you have the special gift tomorrow in church." "You've got to be kidding!" I replied. "Nope, I'm not kidding, says right here . . . Jed, special gift" she said as she pointed at the calendar. There was no use in double checking any place. If it was on the almighty calendar, then it was happening.

My first thought was that I should have switched with someone, but it was a little too late or should I say early in the morning to call someone to switch. My next thought was that

I could just skip it, but that always left a hole in the service. I realized that my only option was to come up with a special gift within the next eight hours. As Keli smiled and said, "I'm going to bed, love you." I walked downstairs to my piano.

You would not think it was that big of deal for a musician with a couple of albums under his belt to whip up a song for church. The problem was, usually when I did a special gift, I tried to pray about it and come up with something that would have some type of message for the congregation. But as I sat there at my piano, nothing came to mind. I messed around a little bit with a few songs, but still nothing. At that point I decided to switch gears in my head. I got up from the piano and went over to my guitar stool. I picked up my Ovation for some reason that evening. That guitar always had special meaning for me. It had been given to me by my buddy, Dan, who had taken his life so many years ago. Each time I played it I always had some special thought of Dan and our early years trying to make it in the music business.

As I sat there and started to strum a little bit I prayed, "Lord, help me find a song tonight that will speak to the congregation tomorrow." With that I started playing. Several songs came and went but then for some reason I settled in on a song entitled, I Am a Servant. It is a great little song, and it just seemed right. The problem was that I had sung it a few years earlier. I hated to sing something again so I thought I would just do it a little different. I put down my guitar and walked back over to the piano. "Maybe I'll just do a piano version of it, which would mix it up a little." I started to play. The song was going ok and I thought it would work, but something still didn't feel right. I thought that maybe I should pick something else, But what?" It wasn't getting any earlier and they wouldn't push church back just because I wasn't ready. This song was just going to have to do!

I decided to play through it one more time. I was finishing up the last verse, but as played I still had a lingering doubt.

This song just wasn't right. "There has just got to be something else that fits tomorrow morning. But what?" Then a voice from behind me said "Play <u>Just a Closer Walk with Thee</u> . . ." I turned to find Clarence standing beside my guitars. "You need to play <u>Just a Closer Walk with Thee</u> tomorrow" he repeated. "I do have that," I thought. I turned to pull a gospel book off the stack of music beside my piano. As I turned back to Clarence he smiled. Placing the book on the piano, I started to play or should I say fumble through it. The truth of the matter is that I am not a very good piano player. I can read music pretty well, but I play mostly by ear. Sight reading was definitely not my specialty. "Play it on the guitar." Clarence said. I turned and he was gone.

Suddenly I did remember that several of my buddies and I had played this song at a gospel jam we used to do on Sunday evenings. Grabbing my guitar, I sat down on my stool, one that had been in my family now for 4 generations, and started to play. It was almost perfect, but something was missing. As I played, I kept hearing the other guys in the jam. It was just better with them playing and singing rather than me as a solo. "That's it," I thought, "The guys will just have to do the song with me tomorrow". So the fact that it was way too late to call anyone to schedule a practice led me to plan one of the most unrehearsed special gifts I had ever sung.

Off to bed I went because I was going to have to get up early!

The next morning I did the chores quickly on the farm and arrived back in the house. I told Keli that she would have to drive to church separately because I needed to get there very early. That wasn't a big deal since we still lived on the same place right around the section from the church. That same church and congregation, that had rescued our things and took us into the flock so many years ago at the time of the fire. She said it was ok and she'd see me at church. I jumped in the shower and then quickly changed into church clothes.

Downstairs I went . . ."Now let me see . . . This one, this one, this one and . . . . of course this one, my Ovation." With four guitars chosen, I made two trips to the truck and off to church I went.

I wanted to get there early so that I could get everything tuned and then hidden under the front pews of the church. After all, no one ever sits in the front pew so the guitars would be out of sight there. The plan was to have the four guitars tuned and ready and then go to my usual unassigned position by the front doors to say good morning to people as they came in. As Bob, Steve, and Randy came in I would let them know that they were helping with the special gift. I had one copy of the music that we would all stand around. I would sing the verses and the guys would all join in and do the harmony during the chorus. Of course, we would all be playing.

I sat there tuning while the church was quiet. Everything went well until the last guitar. It was an old Washburn that I had not played in awhile. It was a great little guitar, but for some reason it had just fallen out of favor in my collection. That being said, the strings had not been changed in awhile. Of course, every guitar player knows what happened next. As I started to bring the strings up to pitch, TWANG! A string broke. "Oh no, not now," I thought. I tried to finish. TWANG! Another string broke. I would just have to replace them all. Quickly I grabbed a new set of strings out of one of the guitar cases I used more frequently and began the task of restringing the old Washburn. The thing about new strings is that it takes them a little bit to settle in. You have to tune and retune several times. So I sat there totally focused on tuning the old Washburn, I had worked my way down to the final E when from the back of the church I heard, "You're still flat." I looked up to see one of the senior members of our church, Donald Gene, sitting in the back of the church. Donald Gene always came into the sanctuary early to just sit and think. He would read through the bulletin and, in my mind, I always thought he was thinking about the sermon title and preparing for the service but I never really knew. "Are you a guitar player, Donald Gene?" I asked "Used to be, a long time ago" the 70+ year old elder replied. "I broke a couple strings and had to put new ones on." I explained. "That will take a bit; you'll have to check it again before you play," he said with all the wisdom of a seasoned guitar player. "I will," was my thankful reply.

I finished tuning the old Washburn and headed for the front door. People were arriving, and I needed to catch the guys on the way in.

The first to arrive was Bob. I said good morning then informed him that he had the special gift today. He promptly informed me that; "no he didn't". I laughed and explained that I needed his help with "Just a Closer Walk with Thee", in the key of G and that he could sing the high tenor part. He remembered doing it at the jam. He agreed but said that he didn't have his guitar. I informed him that I had one for him under the front pew. He smiled and said, "You and your crazy ideas." But he was in!

Steve was the next of the three to show up at the door. He was not too sure about the idea, but after explaining that I wanted to do a quartet and that I badly needed him, he said he was in. He was not going to guarantee anything on the harmonies, but he would give it his best shot. That's all I needed, two down and one to go.

Five minutes before the service and still no Randy! Now that's not unusual for Randy, so I kept waiting. A few minutes passed and the prelude started, still no Randy! "It would be just my luck if Randy wasn't here today," I thought. The service was starting so I had to go. I made my way to the back of the church and met up with Keli; "You go ahead, I'll join you after the special gift," I said "Ok" she smiled as she picked up a bulletin and made her way into the sanctuary. A quick glance at the door still revealed no Randy! "This isn't going to be much of a quartet with only three people. But I guess I am going to have to go with it. After all the church doesn't know what I was planning, I'll just tell them it was a trio," I thought with disappointment. I took one last look at the door because time was getting short. The pastor had started the joys and concerns of the morning. Next would be the Morning Prayer and then we were up. I quickly prayed, "Lord, thank you for the gifts you have given me and let me use them this morning to do your work. Amen" as I looked up something caught my eye. I do not know if it was just a change in movement but my focus had come to land on Donald Gene. Inspiration overcame me.

Boldly I walked up to the last pew on the aisle were Donald Gene sat. "Donald Gene," I said, "I need your help". He looked at me with understanding eyes. I continued "I have a quartet planned for this morning but I am short a singing guitar player. Could you help me out?" "What are you playing?" he asked in a calm voice. "Just a Closer Walk With Thee, in the key of G," I said with hope in my heart. "Yea, I know that one. I'll give it a shot and see if my old fingers can get to the right chords," was his reply. His wife had been listening and put her hand to her mouth. I knew that something special was about to happen.

The Morning Prayer finished and I was on. As I walked forward and placed the microphone and music stand in the required position, I began to talk with the congregation . . . ."This morning I have something special planned for you. Something we have been working on for quite awhile." Bob laughed out loud, I continued "Thank You, Bob for letting the cat out of the bag. Now I have to tell everyone that we have never practiced this song together! As a matter of fact, the guys who are helping me out with this little number didn't even know they were playing this morning until they arrived at church this morning. Oh, well, I guess that leaves room for our mistakes. Last night I had a song I was going to sing for you, but then at the last moment I changed my mind. For some reason I feel like I've been called to sing something else this morning. So this morning I've asked a few guys to help me out with a special quartet. Bob, if you would come on up." Bob walked up and pulled a guitar from under the front pew just as planned. "Steve, if you would come on up" Steve repeated the walk, pulled another guitar from under the pew and positioned himself beside the music stand. "And Donald Gene is going to help me out this morning." The congregation turned to see Donald Gene making his way to the front of the sanctuary. "This morning we are going to be doing an old favorite for you, "Just a Closer Walk with Thee." I turned to pick up the old Washburn from under the pew, but panicked. All that was left was my Ovation. A quick look informed me that Donald Gene had picked up the old Washburn and was already running his fingers over the tuning pegs while comparing notes with Bob and Steve. I smiled, took my position and started in . . . ."I am weak but thou art strong . . . ."

It was an amazing three and a half minutes, four guys playing and singing a wonderful classic. Donald Gene never missed a note, and he sang the harmony like he had written it himself. We finished the song, and the congregation burst into applause. Someone said amen and the preacher stood up to say, "Thank You gentlemen for sharing that wonderful gift with us this morning." As I walked down the aisle to the back of the church, I noticed Donald Gene's wife crying. "Thank You" she whispered, as I walked by. My heart filled with joy.

After church I tried to get around and thank the guys for helping out. It was no problem catching Bob and Steve, but trying to get a word in with Donald Gene was another matter. He was like a rock star in the middle of a fan club. People were patting him on the back. He was hugging people. I overhead another elder say "it was good to see you back up there again." As it turns out, Donald Gene used to play the guitar all the time. Back in the day, he and his brothers use to do quite a bit of singing themselves. When I finally got a chance to talk to his wife she said, "Jed, he used to sing for the kids with his guitar all the time, but he hasn't played at all in over 30 years." When I did get a chance to thank Donald Gene, his reply was like a humble servant's, "Glad I could help out. It was time for me to play again."

As I packed things up and drove home, I couldn't help but think how amazing it could be when you just turned things over to God. Here a special gift that not even 12 hours earlier was even a thought, had made an impact on the lives of many, including my own.

The next day when I was at a local downtown store, the shop owner said that he had heard about our special gift yesterday at the little Brethren Church. When I stopped in at the court house, someone in the clerks' office told me that her mom's friend, who attends our church, said it was the greatest special gift in a long time. Also that night in the canvas shop, Donald Gene's nephew, who attends our church, stopped by and said it was really cool to see his uncle up there singing and playing again. I just couldn't help but wonder in awe how things had worked out.

The following day Keli called me at school with the news. In his retirement Donald Gene worked as a transport driver for a local car dealership. Today on one of his transfer drives, his car had collided with another car on the interstate. Donald Gene had been killed.

"Just a Closer Walk with Thee", now took on an entire new meaning. I hung up the phone and cried.

At the funeral Donald Gene's children told me that our audio guys from church had given the family a copy of Sunday's service. The family talked about how listening while sitting around the kitchen at home had brought them grace. They talked about hearing their dad singing and playing again. It reminded them of a sense of family. The special gift had truly been a gift from God.

As I waited in line to talk with Donald Gene's wife, I kept fumbling around in my head with what I was going to say. No words could ever express what I was feeling. When it was my turn to talk, I didn't need to. She grabbed me and with a hug that felt like I was being held by the Master himself she said, "Thank you! You will never know how much listening to Sunday has meant to this family in our time of need." "God works in mysterious ways," was my initial reply. I went on to find some words that I hoped would be of comfort? But as I walked away, again, she thanked me.

As I left the funeral home, a thought occurred to me. I said to myself, "Clarence is the one that needs to be thanked. It was all his idea!"

"Thanks Clarence."

It was just a few weeks later that I received the following letter from one of Donald Gene's children . . .

> *Dear Jed,*
>
> *We personally want to thank you for listening to the Lord when he led you on Sunday, February 15th. For our father to be there and for you to use him that morning was to me just one more confirmation that the Lord was preparing our father to be called home. It truly was a blessing that the church recorded the service and when we played it at mom's with all my brothers and sisters listening, we could hear our father singing, shedding tears of sorrow and joy. God truly used you that day and we are sure He will use you in many ways to come. Thank you for being obedient to the Lord.*
>
> *In Christ's Love,*
> *Steve and June*

The thing about this sacred journey is that I realize more and more each day how we affect everyone around us. A simple special gift will forever live on in a family. It was just a spur of the moment change on my part, but by having the willingness to listen to my guardian angel and what God wanted, I made a difference.

I sometimes wonder in amazement how God can use us to help each other travel our journeys. We choose to travel roads that give us the opportunities to make a difference in the lives of others. But what really amazes me is the fact that the interconnectedness of situations is a two way street. I realized late one night after I had finished reading the letter from Donald Gene's family that the truth of the matter was that Donald Gene had helped me on my journey. Once again Clarence had come to me in a time of need and provided guidance that would lead everyone forward on the journey. That is the wonderful thing about acknowledging the fact that we can all be a guardian angel to someone and if we are willing to do that, everyone moves forward on the journey.

My first solo album was titled 'The Spirit Will Ride On". The title cut on the album has a verse that goes like this.

> "And I know when life is over
> And I've saddled my last horse.
> And I take that final ride into the sunset.
> The world will be a better place
> Because I choose to ride
> And follow in the footsteps
> That he laid ahead for me . . ."

Somehow, I know that someday when I take that final ride and arrive somewhere farther along the journey, Donald Gene will be there waiting for me. Clarence will probably be standing there beside him. Maybe we will sit down and play a little before we embark farther along this sacred journey.

Epilogue: In His Name

As I continue down this sacred journey called life I realize that with each passing day I learn more and more. I try to keep myself open and aware of what is going on around me and within me. With this awareness comes the sense of how much I have yet to learn.

Clarence has been my guidance in times of need. But mostly he has been a symbol of a greater picture, a sense, that there is a greater spirit. He has solidified in me that some greater connectedness between life as we know it and something bigger is real.

Early on in my life I learned to pray. Growing up in a Christian family meant that praying was just a part of our upbringing. But like most Christians, I became very good at praying and not listening for the answers. After all, where and when does God answer our prayers? It's not like He ever rented a billboard on the local interstate I travel that said "Jed . . . the answer to your morning prayer is . . . ." Clarence has taught me that God does give us answers, but he places them in our hearts for us to find. I've had those feelings in my heart when something was right or wrong but I didn't always listen to them. Sometimes I wasn't listening because I was too busy trying to map out an existence in the hustle and bustle of everyday life. But I have found that even when I was coming home late from a show choir event if I would just take the time to listen, I would find the right thing to do in my heart. Clarence taught me that.

On this journey Clarence has taught me that we need to not only listen for guidance from the angels that God places in out lives. We also need to become the living angels that God needs to work through. After all isn't that the entire message of the Christian faith, "The Golden Rule." Jesus' message was a simple one "do unto others as you would have them do unto you" . . ."For whatever you do for the least of them you do for me."

Clarence has helped me imagine a world in which everyone lived by that rule. Imagine the peace the world would find. That is what God calls us to do, become the angels that continue to serve each other. We need to always look for the good we can do for other people. We need to be the hands of a greater spirit.

Of course being those hands is not always an easy task. However, if we strive to look for the good in the world around us and do all the good we can in spite of the adversities that face us, the journey will be good.

The challenge for me is to try to find a way to convey my own sense of understanding about Clarence and this sacred journey towards a positive collective consciousness.

I remember one day at my desk as I was about to send a mass e-mail to several people in regards to Carrie. I finished the e-mail and was about to sign my name and the final tag . . . Regards, Jed. For some reason I didn't feel it was right . . . Regards just didn't seem to say or sum up what I was thinking. So I hit the back arrow a few times and retyped . . . In Prayer, Jed. That's better I thought and was just about to hit send, but I didn't. Something still didn't feel right . . . In Prayer . . . some of the people reading the e-mail were not believers. Furthermore, it was a formal e-mail going to several school officials and state agencies so I thought maybe I shouldn't get too religious. I hit the back arrow a few more times. Hmmmm . . . maybe just "Sincerely, Jed". That's not right either. It shouldn't be such a big deal how I sign off this e-mail but for some reason it was. I continued to struggle with how to sign off, and sign. I didn't want to come across as a religious nut, but at the same time I wanted people to know and be aware of my faith.

Why was I worried about what people would think? People who knew me were aware of my faith, but yet I didn't want to offend anyone at the same time. Then a voice, from somewhere in the room, or somewhere in my head, a voice from a person that I had come to call Clarence said "If you are doing this in the Lord's name it doesn't matter how you sign off. Just send it." And with that I typed "IHN, Jed".

It wasn't very long before people started responding back. "IHN?" "What does IHN mean?" "Jed Explain IHN?" The e-mails just kept coming and with each one I responded that it simply meant "In His Name" and that for me it just represented the fact that when I do something I try to do it In His Name and in a way that helps everyone along the journey.

I started signing all my e-mails that way, "IHN, Jed". Then I started signing my letters that way. My new album "A Camp Meetin" was coming out so I signed my personal note on the back of the CD case with "In His Name Jed"

People started using IHN for themselves, and I started getting e-mails of thanks for helping people find a way for them to stay connected to their faith in all they do and in every aspect of their life.

Then one day my friend Brian e-mailed me and asked, "Explain this IHN thing to me again" So I did. He replied that he was going to think about it. A few days later I received an e-mail from him in regards to a project that we were working on. He covered all of our business and then at the bottom of his e-mail he signed off with "GIG, Brian" I fired back, "Explain GIG to me, buddy?" His reply was simple "God Is Good, buddy! Thanks for the inspiration." We were both just a little farther along a very sacred journey.

As for me, I know that God is not finished with me yet. I am a work in progress. Clarence has been there for me over and over to remind me that I still have work to do. That is what guardian angels do; they help us along the sacred journey. Yes, each one of us is on a sacred journey. A journey that impacts not only our own lives, but the lives of those around us as well. While on the journey we must listen to the angels among us and discern with our hearts the direction our journeys will take. By walking with Clarence, I have altered my Sacred Journey for the better.

So until we meet again . . . ."Thank You, Clarence!"

IHN Jed

Post Note From The Author

In my travels over the years and around the world I have noticed that there is one thing that never changes from one place to another, the smiles on the faces of the children. Sometimes I can't help but wonder what the world would be like if we could hang on to that simple innocence throughout our lives. What would the world be like if children didn't learn to take on the burdens of their cultures? What if we didn't teach them to hate? What if we didn't teach them to not trust each other? What if we truly taught them to love one another? Wouldn't the world be a better place?

Like many of us, I wake up most mornings and feel myself being pulled in many directions. I try to make the right choices and do the things that will not only be right for me and my family, but also for those that I will come in contact with that day. Some days I do a better job than others but at the end of the day I try and ask myself if I went through the day doing the right thing? Did I live my life that day IN HIS NAME? It is not always easy to walk the path that Jesus did but I do believe it is worth trying each and every day. After all, if we could learn to live our lives by the Golden Rule and treat other people like we want to be treated, wouldn't life be grand? Maybe someday children all over the world would be able to hang on to that simple smile just a little bit longer. Maybe the innocence of youth would last a little longer. Maybe the world would be more aware that we are all HIS children.

Living IN HIS NAME is no guarantee but you know what . . . . It's worth a try!

IHN Jed